THAI TAKI 1

Matt Owens Rees

© Matt Owens Rees 2013 Updated © 2014

Matt Owens Rees has asserted his right under the Copyright Design and Patents Act 1988 to be identified as the author of this work.

No part of this publication may be reproduced, stored in any retrieval system, or transmitted in any form or by any means without prior written permission.

If you enjoyed this book, please encourage your friends to purchase and download their own copy and take a look at its companion volumes: *A Thailand Diary*, *The Thai Way of Meekness*, and *Escape to Thailand*.

Thank you for your support.

Table of Contents

Preface:
    Characters in Order of Appearance:
    Extracts from *A Thailand Diary*:
    Introduction:
Chapter 1: **The Thai Hierarchy**
Chapter 2: **Does *Mai Bpen Rai* always mean Never Mind?**
Chapter 3: **The Thai Smile**
Chapter 4: **Face**
Chapter 5: **Family and Community**
Chapter 6: **The End of a Life**
Chapter 7: **How do Thais see Foreigners?**
Chapter 8: **Sun, Sand, Sea, and Sex**
Chapter 9: **All Thais Cheat**
Chapter 10: **The Thai Mafia**
Conclusion: Piecing together the Thai Jigsaw
Appendix: **Thailand's Political Journey**
About the Author
Free Bonus chapter: *The Thai Way of Meekness*
Glossary of Thai Words

Preface

What is this book about?
It is an up-to-date and balanced exposé of Thais and Thailand.

A fresher look at the differences between the Thai and the Westerner.

A "no holds barred" *take* on the real Thailand that gives an authentic flavour of the country.

Who should read it?
The traveller to Thailand.

Readers who want to learn about the Thais from the comfort of their armchairs.

The expat who has made his home here.

Students studying on cross-cultural courses.

How is it different?
It "tells it as it is" and pulls no punches.

Thai society is explained through real life examples.

The book reveals what really makes the Thai tick.

It shows the Thailand that you may well miss while on holiday.

Often, tourist guidebooks and articles on retiring in Thailand are written with commissions and commercial interests in mind. This is no such book. We do not mislead you into tourist traps. We do not tell you the advantages of staying or retiring here without also discussing the downsides and pitfalls of such a decision.

The ten chapters of *Thailand Take Two* cover the essential differences between Thai and western values and ideas. There is a great deal of material to absorb. Through the characters that are introduced we see there are two distinct worldviews. Accepting that we do not always think the same way as a Thai does, and that we look at life differently sometimes, will help us understand this fascinating country.

Some foreigners assume that a way of life that does not conform to their own cultures or experiences must be deficient or even morally wrong. Such ethnocentric views are put in perspective when we look at how Thais think of corruption and prostitution. Observations about the Thai class system and the eastern concept of face can appear alien to our way of thinking.

Many aspects of what we describe may be familiar to you; some may be unexpected. You may find that you can associate yourself with some of the illustrations given, at other times your experiences may be quite different from those that we have narrated. Because things are not always what they first seem in Thailand you may find some opinions and observations contentious. Only careful scrutiny of Thai activity may allow you to consider the possibility that what you are seeing and hearing are indeed unusual cultural differences common to Thailand.

Although you can skip to the various topics of interest listed in the Table of Contents (you can use the hyperlinks), it is probably best to read the book in chapter order as many features of Thai life are inter-related and depend on an understanding of the key aspects described.

Our sister volume, *A Thailand Diary*, complements this book and describes in a very light style the infinite variety of daily life in Thailand. You will see characteristics such as face, the laid-back lifestyle, and the class system described in detailed personal scenarios involving some of the personalities you have met in *Thailand Take Two*.

Some readers may find it useful to read *Thailand Take Two* and *A Thailand Diary* in parallel. *Thailand Take Two* for the descriptions of the main cultural differences, and *A Thailand Diary* for observing Thais in their day-to-day lives in a way that makes you feel you are actually present at some of the events and situations that are described. For a "fly on the wall" account of an expat's early days in the kingdom, *Escape to Thailand* may be an interesting insight into expat life in the kingdom.

I was asked to write a short volume on Ajarn Ubolwan's doctoral thesis: *The Way of Meekness – Being Christian and Thai in the Thai Way*. Ubolwan is a distinguished Thai academic and her dissertation is worthy of a read in its own right.

University submissions can be heavy reading but Ubolwan highlighted characteristics of the Thai people that are quite similar to those we see in *Thailand Take Two and A Thailand Diary*. It therefore made sense to draw attention to the similarities when writing this 7000 word book.

It now appears in its entirety as a free bonus chapter just before the Glossary of Thai Words.

Characters in Order of Appearance

Ratchanee; a neighbour
    Dao; a university undergraduate
    Goong; a cashier at a photo shop
    Tong; an employee with a problem with her boss
    Geng; a drinking partner
    Colonel Jaran; a Thai colonel, Bancha's boss
    Bancha; a labourer who became a soldier
    Seri; a young lady who had died tragically
    Somchai; a local builder
    Suda; a young lady being interviewed for a job
    Dta Sompet; an 83-year-old Thai
    Suchart; a Thai businessman at LAX airport
    Sakdee; a Thai landlord
    Weelai; a retired Thai university lecturer
    Somrak; a Thai girl married to a foreigner, *farang* in Thai
    Fai; Dta Sompet's divorced younger daughter
    Renu; Faa's youngest daughter, studying in university
    Fon; the wife of Sompet
    Faa; Sompet's eldest daughter
    Damrong; a teacher and relative of Sompet
    Ning; Faa's daughter, working in Bangkok
    Adoon; a banker in Chiangmai
    Lek; a bargirl
    Somporn; a *farang's* girlfriend
    Pranom; a senior university lecturer

Mana; a Thai student caught cheating
Names have been changed to protect individual privacy.

Extracts from A Thailand Diary

9 January

Murder most foul.

Our *soi* (lane) is single track, so we could not get the car out when the police vehicle parked outside our neighbour's house. And you don't ask armed police officers, anywhere in the world, to move their car for you. They park where they want to park.

A crowd had started to gather outside the house. The locals wanted to know what was going on, and they were waiting around to gather whatever snippets of information or gossip were available.

Ratchanee told me that one of the brothers in the house was dead. There had been some heavy drinking the night before and the men's mother had heard some shouting downstairs. She had thought nothing of it. In the morning, the mother found her son lying in a pool of blood.

The police were now investigating a murder. They will start searching for two Burmese.

The brothers drank regularly with the same group of friends from neighbouring *sois*, all Thai nationals. Not my type, but friendly enough. I'd never seen any Burmese, legal or illegal, in the area, and neither had anyone else.

The police didn't stay long and the family immediately started to clean the house and tidy the garden. Monks come round quickly after a death in Thailand in order to start the funeral rites, and it's best that everything is spotless before they arrive.

We may learn more about what happened in the coming days. More likely, we will not.

15 February

It is a nice touch that members of the Thai royal family give out degree certificates to graduates at the universities. Very few countries do that.

Dao invited us to the rehearsal.

She had got up at 5am to get her hair styled and her face made up. Thais are always careful about their appearance and Dao is an attractive young lady. Today she looked like a film star. She had called the dummy run "the walking" and I could see why. All the students lined up and walked up to the stage where a stand-in handed out the certificates. This was repeated until they got it absolutely right. Yes, it was a day of much walking.

On the day that the degree is conferred, the students' families and friends join in the celebrations, flowers and gifts are showered on the new graduates, and many photographs are taken with fellow students and teachers.

16 March

Picked five large bunches of bananas this morning and gave three to my neighbours. I have more than enough for the next few weeks. Sharing what you have is very much a Thai way. It shows *nam jai* (generous giving). Everyone in the *soi* is forever giving fruit, plants, and vegetables to one another. If there's no one at home, they'll put a bag of goodies on your gatepost.

27 April

I can count on the fingers of one hand the number of times I have forgotten to fasten my seatbelt. Even if it was not a legal requirement in Thailand, I would "clunk, click, every trip" as I would if I was driving in my home country.

I'm going to have to give you a ticket. I saw you put your seatbelt on after you came round the corner.

Pom jai ngern hai khun dio nee. Taorai na kap. (Can I pay you now? How much?)

My wallet was 400 baht lighter, but I was not given a ticket. I had my licence back. The police officer halted the traffic to allow me to pull out, gave an even smarter salute than before, and I was on my way.

Collecting minor fines in this way is common practice. The money is shared out later at the station. It's regarded as a perk of the job and really forms part of officers' salaries.

4 May

Kawp krua gawn; peuan gawn.
Family first; friends first.

Had to get some passport photos taken today. Took my queue ticket and sat down to wait, and wait, and wait.

Goong, one of my neighbours, was the cashier on duty and when she saw me, she called me over to her colleague on the photo booth. Four minutes later and everything was finished.

I do not like this pulling of rank that goes on so much here; but there was little I could do. Would have been insulting to refuse the fast tracking. Goong would have lost face in front of her colleagues. The main point, however, is that no one minded; it was seen as quite normal and acceptable for family and friends not to have to wait in line.

23 June

I suggested that Tong ask for a meeting with her boss about the delays to her vacation approval and more importantly her job evaluation.

That would seem like a challenge to my boss's position, Matt. Everyone has a place in the office hierarchy. I will get some colleagues to drop a few well-chosen comments about my work and how it compares with the performance of others; but I can do no more than that. Thais like to use an intermediary to resolve a problem rather than going direct. I know that sounds strange to Westerners, Matt.

15 July

Watched police checking for illegals on a building site. One elderly woman worker did not have her Thai ID card with her. By law, you must carry these cards with you at all times. Rules are rules.

Law enforcement is flexible in Thailand. It was obvious from her appearance that she was Thai. And, out of respect for an older person, the police were not going to make a fuss. She was asked to sing the Thai national song to prove her nationality.

http://www.youtube.com/watch?v=djwY41a4lsA

(Ctrl and click will normally work or you can type the link into your internet browser)

12 September

Saw Tim for lunch today. Work is proceeding well on his house build. They have started making the concrete base and building up the outside walls. The men are doing the heavy work but the women are busy pulling the carts containing the made-up cement to where most of it is needed. The supervisor is watching and making sure the block work is being laid straight and level. One of the workers had started on the second course without cutting the first block in half. The result was that the second course was not being staggered. The join should never be above another join as that takes away the strength of the wall.

Tim saw it and quietly told the worker's boss. He was right not to get angry and make a big fuss about it, and it was better that he told the boss and not the worker. The supervisor would not have liked that. He is in charge and only he gives the orders. Status is all-important in Thailand and no one must lose face. Tim emigrated from America two months ago and is learning fast that interacting with people in Thailand is not the same as in the West.

9 October

Imitate the humour style of your host country. Break the ice first and watch the body language of those you are with. You may still get it wrong but it won't be disastrous.

"Pai nai kap" (where are you going?), I shouted as Geng got up from the table where we were all sitting and drinking cold pints of the local brew. Thais tend to just get up and go without any explanation. I found it strange at first.

We all knew where he was going when he walked towards some bushes in the garden. We were having a reasonably heavy drinking session, so it was not difficult to guess. He turned round, laughed, and went on to water the shrubbery.

That sort of joke would go down well in France. Other countries may be more serious. It would not even raise a snigger in Russia, but your attempts at another type of humour would bring the house down. The rule holds true: be careful telling a joke if you are unaware of the culture of your listeners and their reactions to humour.

14 November

Not to everyone's liking, but northern Thai food can become an acquired taste. Dishes are served with an extensive range of different spices and herbs. Variety is in; blandness is out.

You select the food you want and put a little on your own plate. Or, more typically, someone on your table will serve you, particularly if you are older than the others are.

Sticky rice is the staple food of choice in the north. You roll some up in a ball with your hand and then envelop it around whatever food you wish to eat. Your right hand is always used, never the left, which is reserved for toiletry purposes in eastern countries.

(Sticky rice is called *kao niao* –*kao,* rice; *niao,* sticky. And not to be confused with *kee niao,* which is Thai slang for stingy or mean, literally sticky shit).

28 November

The snake sunning itself beside the pond was not a cobra but it was about two metres long nevertheless. I was not going to go near it and tried to get the dogs to move away.

Unless cornered, snakes will normally keep out of your way. Just be careful if walking in long grass that you don't accidentally disturb them.

Some snakes have keen eyesight; others do not. This is why you often see them moving their heads from side to side to get better focus. They sense movement from any ground vibration when you try to walk away. The best advice is to stand still, hold your breath, and not make any sharp change of direction.

If you don't pose a threat to a snake, it may slide away.

Make a mental note of its colour and other distinguishing features. If you are bitten or sprayed with venom, it would become important information for the hospital in its choice of serum.

If their young are threatened, you could be in a dangerous and tight spot. Snakes have been known to chase a car that has driven over a snake's batch of eggs.

Having said that, you are more likely to encounter snakes in their professional capacity in lawyers' offices than anywhere else.

5 December

Today is a national holiday as it is the King's birthday. It is also Father's Day in Thailand. Tens of thousands of people, many having camped out overnight, have gathered in Sanam Luang Park in Bangkok to cheer the monarch as he passes. All one could hear was the crowd crying out "Long live our King. Long live our King." Many with tears in their eyes. King Bhumibol is much loved by his people; having reigned since 1946, he is the only king most Thais have ever known.

Of course, in the West there would be singing, dancing, and drinking. Any excuse for a party. What is striking in Thailand, and what sets it apart from many other countries, is the passionate and patriotic fervour that goes with it.

You would party in America to celebrate Independence Day; the monarch's jubilees are fun events in the UK. But you would not hear "God Bless America" and "God Save the Queen" at private parties.

Thailand is different. Workers on the construction site opposite are still partying. The sounds of *Sawng Phra Ja Rern, Sawng Phra Ja Rern* (Long live our King) are ringing out constantly from every house in the village. And it's well past midnight.

28 December

My name is Waterfall, call me Water.

Thais only use surnames for official documents. Even the Thai prime minister is called by her first name. Your boss may be called *wanna* (boss) or *pee* (a word meaning elder), followed by the first name, never the surname.

To confuse even more, Thais have two first names – a nickname and an official name.

A nickname is selected at birth by the parents. A small baby may be called *Goong*, (shrimp) or *Lek* (tiny).

Thais can be very superstitious. Nicknaming your child *Oun* (fat) or *Moo* (pig) is supposed to discourage and frighten ghosts and evil spirits, and dissuade them from any association with the newly born child.

The official name is registered some days later at the local district office, usually after a monk has been consulted over the choice of name. The parents simply give the monk (the proper word is actually *Bikkhu* in Thai) the time and day of his birth and he will decide a name. His suggestion will invariably be accepted.

So, from now on, I will call Waterfall by his nickname, *nam*, water.

Introduction

Oh, East is East and West is West
And never the twain shall meet

Is Kipling right?

When Rudyard Kipling wrote those words, he was making the point that Westerners, whether travellers or expats, do not easily integrate into the ways of an eastern society.

However, he went on to conclude that the people of two cultures could indeed absorb the traditions and life styles of other countries provided that they have the will to do so. The *twain* can meet. Those from the East and the West can come together, communicate with each other, and will find no trouble in doing so.

They looked each other between the eyes, and there they found no fault.

Kipling correctly summarised the difficulties and frustrations of living in a different national culture from one's own; and was right to say that it was certainly not impossible to bridge the cultural divide. Both those who come as travellers to visit the country and those who have made Thailand their home can try to understand and appreciate the differences between people from other societies.

If the Thais and the émigrés both adopt a little give and take, living together will be more harmonious and satisfying. The Westerner will find that he is living rather than existing.

There is a good reason why this book is called *Thailand Take Two*. In the same way that Kipling turned the much-quoted phrase *never the twain shall meet* on its head by saying that the opposite is in fact true; this book suggests that we all *take* a different approach on Thailand in an attempt to understand the Thai better.

Put on hold for a moment the stories you may have read or heard about this country.

Let us take a fresh look, a second *take*, at the reality that is Thailand.

We will explore together the differences between Thai and western cultures. You will meet the real Thai, people like *Lek, Adoon, Weelai, and Suchart*. The bargirl and the banker, the teacher and the well-heeled traveller. You will discover parts of this country and its national culture that may well surprise you.

Thailand Take Two is an impartial, honest, and balanced view of the country and its people, showing both faces of The Land of Smiles – a Thailand that is neither a perfect paradise on earth nor a dangerous den of dishonesty and deviousness.

The tendency to avoid arguments and to adopt a hassle-free lifestyle is what you will probably notice quite quickly about the Thais. You would not be wrong. *Thailand Take Two* goes into some detail on these themes from several angles. We will look at cheating, corruption, the idea of face, and even the sex trade; and we will note how inter-related these and other concepts are.

Thais can be obsessed about apparent slights or snubs. Shouting, raising one's voice, arguing however logically, criticising in front of others; all can be a formula for disaster in your relationships with a Thai. This book will thrash out these characteristics and offer some ideas for compromise, some ways for the *twain* to meet.

The Thais have a strong community spirit. You will see their eagerness to help others. I shall share with you some stories of the Thai family circle and demonstrate what really influences the Thais in their daily lives.

There is also a strong class structure and we will illustrate some of the "unwritten" rules of hierarchy that are second nature to a Thai. Because it highlights everything that happens in Thailand, we will describe many examples of how hierarchy works in our first chapter before we move on to other aspects of Thai life style.

Every man, woman, and child knows his or her place in society. It is a stabilising factor. There are accepted and unchangeable conventions to establish the pecking order. The ideas of respect for elders and betters, and the noblesse oblige concept are absolute in Thailand. *Thailand Take Two* will compare them with western values.

However, before we do that, let us look at first impressions.

On holiday, we enjoy the friendliness of the smiling people, the warm weather, the eye-catching scenery and coastline, and the *mai bpen rai* (laid-back) attitude to life. It is not something we experience that often in the West.

We appreciate the colourful cultural shows of music and dance, the varied styles and splendour of the temples, and the diversity of regional life outside Bangkok. Do we always see the real Thailand away from the tourist spots? Do we get to know Thai people and understand why they are so unlike us?

As visitors, we put up with the minor nuisance of a tourist tout telling us that the Temple of the Emerald Buddha is closed for essential repairs but that his brother owns a good gem shop nearby. We tolerate being charged higher prices than the locals in many places. Sometimes we see through the white lies we are told and sometimes we do not. We wonder why we get evasive answers to some of our questions. Is it Thai shyness or is there some deeper reason?

Reading *Thailand Take Two* will enable you to distinguish between the myths and the realities of Thailand. It is not only sun, sand, sea, and sex. Lying and dishonesty will be put in perspective. Avoiding arguments and quarrels are Thai traits that you will not be slow to recognise. Walking away from a tricky and uncomfortable situation is, as well as saving face, a way to avoid conflict. It makes for a pleasant *mai bpen rai* attitude and a relaxed lifestyle. However, it can become problematic if the situation involves a foreigner.

This book will give you some hints of the essential character of Thais and Thailand. You will see the words face, hierarchy, family, community, *mai bpen rai*, no conflict, *sanuk* (fun), and freedom appear in several chapters: sometimes in a lighthearted way, sometimes in more depth. These are all indispensable ingredients of Thailand's enigmatic pot pourri. A real mix of different ideas, thoughts, concepts, and attitudes.

I hope you enjoy Thailand and meeting the typical Thai. I sincerely hope you enjoy *Thailand Take Two*.

Chapter 1

The Thai Hierarchy

Why are you here today, soldier?
Because I was told to be here, sir.

That was a perfect answer to Colonel Jaran's blunt question. Bancha had only been in the Thai army for two months, but he knew how to talk to superiors. He knew how to obey orders.

Whether in the army or not, many Thais, depending on their place in the Thai hierarchy, would just obey. Questioning would not be an option for them.

The "rules" are reinforced in the family and in the schoolroom. Children call their elders *pee* and father and mother are always referred to as *mae* or *paw*, never by anything else. Heated arguments in a family are almost unheard of. I have never heard a son or daughter answer parents back.

The three-year stint in the Thai army, mandatory for almost all Thais, is a further powerful influence on preserving this class structure and instilling a sense of discipline and subservience.

There are no written guidelines explaining how they must conform to their particular position within the class system. Everyone knows which rung of the ladder he or she stands on. There are implied conventions that underline everything that happens in Thailand. That is why it is important to consider this topic before any other feature of Thai life.

Thais dislike any change from the norm. They feel safe when their precise place in society, in the class system, is secure and transparent to all with whom they come into contact.

Class, age, and perceived wealth are very significant to Thais. They feel more at ease if they know where you stand relative to them in the social order. This explains why, if they cannot get clues from the clothes that you are wearing, they will ask how old you are, where you were educated, and what you do for a living.

The carrying out of an action or a command without question is imperative. A soldier often has to react quickly and without thinking. Lives could be lost if he hesitated, discipline is important. Questioning an order from a superior is not acceptable and disobeying could be a court martial offence. A soldier can in some circumstances suggest that there is a better solution to carrying out an express order, though he would have to do so tactfully and with respect. Using initiative does not come naturally to a Thai. They regard it as showing that they are acting out of their proper station or place in society.

As anyone who has been an ordinary soldier knows, it is not easy to find a means of telling an officer that his judgment may be a tad impractical or show signs of naivety without causing offence or, worse, being put on a charge. The officer's analysis of a situation may defy logic in the minds of more experienced soldiers who have been closer to real action.

There is nothing more dangerous than a newly commissioned officer, straight out of training, consulting a map when seasoned men have already assessed the situation and are ready to move. Thailand has its fair share of such men in power, both inside and outside the military. The class system, the hierarchy, enables those with money, influence, and position to be put into senior appointments. Merit and ability is not always evident. It can cause frustration with subordinates but they never show it.

Every day in the workplace, Thais appear to be submissive to what the boss wants them to do. You will more often hear them saying, "I was ordered to do this" rather than "I was asked to do this." There is total outward respect for someone of a higher class or position. If you watch carefully, you will see that they know their station in life. They do as they are told.

The subordinate will be very cautious about carrying out an action not specifically requested. He will be uneasy in offering any alternative plan. Any proposal that is made will be made with a liberal measure of tact and meekness. The boss will never be put in a position where he may appear wrong or lose face.

From his early childhood, through school, and when Bancha was employed as a labourer on a building site, he understood the unwritten rules of Thai hierarchy. He knew he had to submit to his elders and to those higher up the social scale. His parents and teachers had taught Bancha that he must know his place.

Thai people are aware of the limitations that are created by their rank in society. They learn the principles of hierarchy early in their lives. Those lower down the social scale learn that they must obey their superiors and elders. The junior person in the hierarchy is more subservient and will almost always do without question what the senior expects of him. Saying "no" is often not a choice available to the ordinary Thai.

Their love of show is born of necessity. They need you to know their status, importance, and authority in society. It starts at an early age. At a local school fete, I saw several uniformed schoolgirls around 11 or 12 years of age directing cars in the school car park. It was a sensible attempt to get vehicles parked neatly and in their correct positions. But did it really need a lot of whistle blowing and waving of arms? Even at that young age it appeared to be an example of their need to show authority.

Some Thais will show off their uniforms, fine clothes, and expensive jewellery, even on occasions when it is not appropriate to do so. We see later, in *The End of a Life*, how Thais deal with such presumptuous people. Whether they are car park attendants in the shopping malls, workers in some commercial organisations, or bank employees; staff will wear their uniforms with pride to show the value of the job they are doing. Thais believe it is important that you are aware of their position and authority over you.

Members of parliament, local government officers, and the village headmen, all have white uniforms to wear on ceremonial or official duties.

That said, you will meet many high-ranking Thais who wear their formal white dress only as a badge of office and they would never think of taking advantage of their status or seniority. Like the ordinary Thai, they are the nicer people to be with.

Important government functions require attendees to wear full ceremonial dress. Resplendent in their starched meticulously ironed white uniforms, they indeed present an impressive sight marching or standing to attention. However, I noticed at a recent event that not everyone was wearing their entire entitlement of ribbons and medals. Times are changing. Yes, the white uniforms will remain obligatory and the Thais will still wear them. The new generation, including teachers and government workers, do not use the occasion to impress. They wear only what they believe is the minimum formal dress that tradition demands.

In 2013, female students in some northern universities had some limited success in getting the authorities to change their rigid uniform rules. They can now wear clothes more becoming young ladies in their late teens and early twenties. Still dressed in white blouse and black skirt, they do have some freedom in choosing the particular fashion that best suits them as individuals.

The Thais talk a lot about those they refer to as "hi-so." Some they respect; some they do not. The people believe in and respect class classifications if they are genuine. Good doctors and teaches are well liked. They do not appreciate those that show off deliberately and make out they are better than others in an offensive way. Successful business people, often Thai-Chinese from well-established families, hardly ever flaunt their wealth. Like the ordinary Thai, they can integrate well with foreigners. It is those in the middle, those with new money, who may prove less easy to get to know as they are inclined to think they are more superior than they actually are.

Technically, the word "hi-so" refers to members of high-ranking families and the status is obtained only at birth. Thais talk of them as being "the higher." They are often patrons of good works and they can be regarded as leaders and role models to whom people can look up. They provide psychological encouragement to communities. Many are third or fourth generation Chinese immigrants in the business or political community. Invariably, a hi-so name implies wealth.

A surname which is a place name preceded by *"na"* indicates a distant descendant of royalty or nobility. For example, *na Chiangmai* tells you the person has a distinguished and powerful background, usually traceable to the former Lanna royal family. The equivalents in Europe are names such as *von Trapp* or *de Vigny*.

Those with new money, the nouveau riche, who can afford to live a trendy lifestyle are not of the same upper class. While they are still regarded with some awe because of their riches and influence, they are not genuinely liked by the average Thai. In fact, the term "hi-so" has become derogatory because so many of them have forgotten that with position and privilege come a social responsibility to those of lesser fortune.

A group of around twenty graduates, mainly in their mid-forties, attended a funeral of a fellow student, Seri, who had tragically met an early death. One was an entrepreneur who travelled extensively worldwide, another ran her family palm oil business, another held a relatively minor job in government, yet another was a college professor. Seeing them together, you could not have determined who had money and who had not. They would not have regarded themselves as "hi-so" and were not displaying their success in life or in anyway showing off.

The élite, at the top of the ladder of hierarchy, accept their own obligations to society, to the community. Noblesse Oblige has duties as well as privileges. The senior person may be a prominent local employer providing work, and therefore some financial security for those in the community. He may use his contacts and influence to assist in resolving minor problems that his employees get into. He may well help financially in times of family hardship. Support and advice is repaid by employee loyalty, though Thais would not regard that as a permanent obligation. You would still outwardly respect a boss that has been demoted but you would no longer owe him any loyalty and you may take opportunities to gossip about him. Maybe getting one's own back for when you had to bite your tongue in conversations with him.

Although social distance is maintained, a bond develops between boss and worker. Similar bonds exist between teacher and student, elder and junior. It is part of the fabric of Thai society. They will not, though, be close friends. The boss is always the boss.

A Westerner sees many enigmas in Thai culture. Students will respect and follow a teacher's rulings in school or university. Questioning is neither expected nor thought to be correct etiquette. Student activists can, on the other hand, be enthusiastic and forceful in making their views on social and political issues known. Teachers won't intervene but feel a strong responsibility towards them and a little let down by their activities. Their relationship with their students means they accept they are somewhat blameworthy for the actions of their students. On the one hand, teachers see unswerving respect from them; on the other, there is an unwelcome sense that the rules of hierarchy are not being followed. The obligation to be both a boss to be obeyed and a caring and beneficent mentor is an unusual dichotomy for

Westerners to grasp. In Thailand, whether the person is a patron, a boss or a teacher, he is forever identified as the "superior."

Local community projects and the local *wat* (temple) benefit widely from the largesse of the super rich. And whom you know can be very useful in Thailand.

In this country the rich and the not so well off depend on each other. It makes for a cohesive society, even if it appears a little undemocratic at times. But at a distance. Classes do not easily mix, whether in Thailand or elsewhere, unless there is the natural bonding that we saw, for example, when graduates attended their friend Seri's funeral.

The ordinary Thais will keep a low profile when dealing with the élite, *the rich men in their castles*, as it were. They certainly will not tangle with any powerful criminal gangs, syndicates, or those in powerful positions. They bond within their own class.

The way you dress can indicate your standing in the eyes of others. Thais judge you by what you are wearing and place greater emphasis on that than on anything else about you.

Your views and ideas will fall on deaf ears if you dress scruffily or do not "look the part." Thais look for credibility. More often than not, the clothes you wear will determine how they react to you and how they treat you.

On a comment on Christian missionaries, the Thai academic, Dr Ubolwan, highlighted that the Thai is more responsive to the messenger than the message. If the western missionary, the messenger, does not make an impression on the Thai by his general appearance and bearing, then he can forget trying to get the message across. Thais view you largely from first contact.

A farang goes into a Ferrari dealership and looks at the top of the range model. He's dressed in jeans and an open T-shirt. He's virtually ignored by the salesman who is neither treating him seriously nor answering his questions about the car. He walks out of the showroom and jumps into his Porsche; the salesman is kicking himself because he has lost commission on a potential sale. It would have been better to have listened to the customer and established a rapport with him.

This well-known story may well be fictional but it illustrates how Thais can misjudge a *farang* (white foreigner) because they do not understand that a Westerner does not always parade his wealth for all to see. To many Thais, it seems logical that if you have money or position, you make sure other people know it.

To sell his goods, a salesperson must understand his customer's needs and his background. The early missionaries failed to copy that technique. One of the reasons for their lack of success in Thailand was they did not appreciate what a Thai wants from a preacher. They spoke to their "flock" without understanding their needs. Thais want emotional reasons to believe in a concept. They like to be persuaded by examples. The other reason was a failure to understand Thai culture.

On occasion, there is a fine line between a Thai wanting to dress expensively to show his position in society, and the Thai that regards himself as better than others and is doing so merely to show off.

How you dress helps them decide whether they should *wai* you first and whether to call you *pee* (if older) or to use a particular title to show respect. Being inquisitive about you was never further from their minds. Who *wais* whom is determined mainly by class. You do not *wai* a servant. Thais will, however, *wai* foreigners who are thought to have money even if the Thai knows he is not of a high class or background. Tiger Woods, who is of mixed Thai/American blood, is accorded a *wai* because of his golfing prowess and his American background. If he were an average golfer like the rest of us, he would not be so accepted in an élite golf club in Thailand. The fervent nationalism of the Thai sometimes smacks of xenophobia.

If you listen to a Thai conversation between a superior and an assistant, you will notice that the subordinate's responses can be limited to *kap, kap, kap.* (yes, yes, yes.) No questioning, no dialogue, the instructions will be followed. You can always sense who the puyai (superior) is and who has the lower status (the *punoi*.) No Thai honestly believes he is equal to the next man. He willingly accepts that some people are better than he is and some are inferior.

Perhaps that takes away a little of his personality.

Krap is the polite word (or particle) used by male speakers at the end of a sentence. It normally has no meaning, though in the context above it meant "yes." A female subordinate would say *ka* and a male might often offer a smattering of *krapom* as well, showing even more respect.

(As with many oriental peoples, the Thais tend to pronounce an 'r' as an 'l' or not at all. So the technically correct *krap* (with its rather unfortunate connotation for western listeners) softens to *kap* more times than not.)

When you hear only *krap, kap,* or *ka* as responses, whether in the military or in any other social situation, you will know that the Thai speaker is only carrying out orders as expected. Doing as he is told. The position in the chain of command is perfectly understood and respected by both parties. The hierarchical structure is not flexible and tradition dictates that the unrecorded rules established centuries ago are tacitly understood.

Thais would never refuse outright to carry out an order from a superior or a member of the privileged classes. They may perhaps find an excuse not to comply. They would never cause offence by saying "no" to one's face. That would be unacceptable to the Thai, be emotionally upsetting, and to be avoided. Westerners cannot change that thinking but we can try to understand it. Cultures are different throughout the world.

You may notice class distinctions as you travel through Thailand. Northerners, those from the province of Isaan, and the hill-tribes are often looked down on by the richer city dwellers of Bangkok.

There are divisions based on hierarchy on the island of Phuket between the *chao lay* (sea gypsies, from *chao* person, *talay* sea) and local landowners. The sea gypsies regard themselves as Thai as they have lived in these coastal regions for over 300 years. They have their own language, etiquettes, and they subscribe to the animist religion. They do not readily join in with other Thais.

As they have no legal papers to the land they occupy, there are continuing problems with developers who want to build profitable tourist facilities. The government tries to find compromising solutions but can do little to solve the basic problem of there being such wide class differences between the *chao lay* and the property developers.

Thai attitudes to communism and colonialism are linked to their understanding of how the class system operates in Thailand.

Thai hierarchy was so strong that communism found no foothold in the country. Workers felt unable to take a strong stance against the élite. The influence of the two concepts of family and community on a Thai, as we see in a later chapter, was stronger than the principles of any political party. Thais knew their rôle in life and felt secure in that knowledge. They were fearful of the unknown consequences of communism. To accept it, or even to consider it, would have meant questioning the status quo and it is not a national trait to do that.

Communism tries to appeal to a person's perceived lowly station in life and to a notion of fairness and equality. Thais follow their hearts and not their heads. They listen to their emotions, what they feel. Personal loyalties are fundamental to a Thai and they need to experience a sense of belonging to family and community and not a belonging to a cause. Thais will compromise; communists, with more entrenched ideas of the palpably evident rights of their cause, will not. Pragmatism and the need to live contentedly in a land with sharp separations between classes outweigh any thoughts of looking at the principles of a political party. Thais don't question. They did not want to step out of what they believed was their dictated position in life.

Most Thais followed their emotions and, conscious of their position in the social order, rejected those cold rational political ideas, however logically the proponents of communism had put their arguments.

The rigid hierarchy and the strong patriotic fervour of the Thai did not sit well with ideas of colonisation. It partly explains why Thailand was never formally colonised. The country did however benefit from the work of the many doctors, engineers, and other professionals who came as expats or on short tours of duty.

When Japan invaded in the Second World War the Thais capitulated out of pragmatism within a few days and declared war on the Allies. By some definitions, therefore, it cannot be said that the country was never colonised by a foreign power.

Over the last 400 years there had been much immigration from China, mainly by the Han Chinese. Those of Chinese origin heavily populated the upper class, big business, and government. Two Chinese immigrant brothers formed the largest private company in Thailand, the CP group, in 1921. Its net worth is equivalent to between 5% and 10% of Thailand's gross domestic product. Because many businesses in Thailand are family-run, one sees a great deal of nepotism in the country. In politics, family members are given key jobs. The Shiniwatra family has provided three Thai prime ministers. Many of the networks – and we discuss this later – are from Chinese backgrounds.

Nowadays, their families have fully assimilated into Thai life. They have complete Thai citizenship. They are prominent in business and government and keep many Chinese traditions. We should perhaps refer to them as Thai-Chinese. I once asked a prominent business owner whether she thought of herself as Thai or Chinese. She took her time in answering but said, "I have a Thai ID card. I am Thai" But her body language and delay in replying said it all.

The French empire-building ambitions of the 19th century left a nasty taste in the mouths of many Thais. It is no coincidence that a white foreigner became known in Thai as a *farang* from the adjective *farangset* (French).

Even today, particularly amongst the older generation, there is an uneasy feeling about foreign powers trying to colonise other countries; trying to "westernise" them (the white man's burden, as Westerners described it in the context of other colonisations.) Some Thais still think that *farangs* can occasionally come across as condescending and even racist, trying to impose their ideas and western customs. They invariably believe that foreigners are all extremely wealthy.

Thais do not like hearing any criticism about their country, and a Westerner making too direct a comparison with the West in an attempt to change a Thai's way of thinking will never succeed in doing so. To get your point across you would need to use a lot of persuasion, but more fundamentally, you should try to express your ideas in terms of their own experiences and not yours.

We all cheer and root for our national team to win, whatever the sport. Sometimes, English football fans, for example, go over the top in shouting abuse at the opposing foreign team, and even getting violent. Generally, however, western nationals can be patriotic and supportive of their team without any incidents being caused.

Thailand is not the same. Although there are separate words in the language for patriotism and xenophobia, in practice no distinction is made. They do not like anyone making a criticism of themselves or their country.

In Thai schools and universities, there is a strong sense of hierarchy. You can see this when you observe children and students listening to teacher but seldom asking questions or thinking critically or constructively. It is almost as if the teacher is infallible and always regarded as being right. The same way that western teaching methods fifty years ago showed the same signs of unswerving acceptance of what teacher said. In fact, you may observe many parallels between Thai life today and your recollections of life in the West during the less prosperous years after the Second World War.

I am sure you will note also that Thais, whenever they meet you, ask a great deal of questions. Where are you going? Are you having fun? How old are you? That is being sociable and friendly. Questioning to get information or making comments, particularly to more senior people, is not a feature of their lifestyle.

Students who feel more confident, and want to find out more about their subject, may ask a question in class, but there is always that inbred reluctance to challenge or criticise. Great care will be taken to phrase a question or make a comment in ways that are neither disrespectful, nor sarcastic, nor challenging. The phrase, "I think you are wrong, teacher," which might be permitted in a western classroom, would not be tolerated in Thailand.

If a teacher quoted a wrong source, a student might more courteously say:

Is it also true, Ajarn, that some people, some text book writers, have suggested that it was Isaac Newton who gave us the theory of universal gravitation and the three laws of motion?

No loss of face, no challenge to the hierarchy, no presumption that a war of words was about to develop. The teacher would not feel that the student was challenging her position. She would respond positively to the question. If, however, she replied, "that is not true," the student would give in and not argue the point. The student would have tried subtly and politely to put her point of view to her ajarn, her professor. She would not be able to do more.

Academic gowns are no longer worn in the classroom but students will *wai* and bow their heads whenever they see their teachers. It is not uncommon for a pupil to stand while addressing a teacher and to wait outside the classroom door until permission is given to enter.

Some educators are encouraging more critical appraisal from their classes, often because they themselves have had some exposure to western educational methods. They try to encourage students to think for themselves and challenge ideas in a way their parents would never have dreamed of doing. Rote learning and accepting whatever is written in a textbook without too much discussion is, however, still prominent.

If you telephone a secretary in the West and leave a message for a superior (a serious complaint, say) it will usually be relayed. Apart from being normal business practice, it covers the secretary if the problem escalates and her manager had not been informed. A Thai secretary may appear to forget to pass the message on and need to be reminded.

It is not a case of forgetfulness or laziness. It is an example of the Thai easygoing style of life, the concept of *mai bpen rai*. She is trying to save face for her boss by not relaying an unwelcome message. Nobody likes to be the messenger of bad tidings. In a highly stratified society such as Thailand's, it is difficult for a subordinate to give bad news to a superior. Thais do not like unpleasant argument. If she does indeed eventually pass on the message, she would find it uncomfortable to do so.

In the office environment, the word *wanna* (boss) is regularly used when talking to or referring to the person in charge. Using words like these, Thais show that they are aware of where people fit into the class system. In nineteenth century England, "sir" was used a lot. In upper class society, a son or daughter would have called their father "sir." Even today, you would always refer to your doctor as "doctor" but you would not be as deferential or formal with your boss as possibly your parents or grand parents would have been.

You can respect authority while still being on first name terms in the West. In Thailand, you would need to use more formally correct forms of address. Ajarn Weelai, Colonel Jaran, Khun Manat. You would keep a respectful distance from your superiors or betters. I recall labouring in a steel mill and calling the boss "Mr. Smith" in the factory but "John" in the pub after work. You would never do that in Thailand.

You can sense that Thai workers enjoy the camaraderie that is found in their workplaces and other group situations. For them, work needs to be fun (*sanuk*.) If it is not, they leave. If they feel unaccepted – by the boss, for example – it can make them lose some confidence and self-esteem. They often back down when confronted with a more senior person. That can mean a loss of face and they then question their own abilities. A Thai will cover that with a smile, but deep down there is bound to be some resentment. It is in these cases that you will hear *krap, krap, krap* and little else being repeated.

Titles are important in Thailand and are widely used. A retiree of any profession retains his title. One would say Colonel Jaran even after he is retired. University professors and lecturers are called a*jarn* together with their first name; schoolteachers are called *kroo* followed by their first name. You call doctors *maw*, or rather *khun maw*, which shows the right level of respect. The use of rank both inside and outside the place of work shows that these titles are key indicators of a person's position in the hierarchy. The social order is being reinforced.

In the West, one would tend to agree with what a doctor says.

Yes, doctor. Yes, doctor.

Assuming he must be right. They like patients using their titles. In France, the mayor is always called Monsieur le Maire. Monsieur l'Agent for the police.

Similarly, in Thailand, you will hear titles being used all the time. It shows the respect that is owed to superiors, whether merited or not.

Since surnames are only infrequently used in Thailand, giving a person's title or profession helps identify him. Builder Somchai is often referred to as *Chang* Somchai. Better still if you emphasise his position as a skilled worker by a judicious use of *geng*, (clever, skilful), when commenting on his work, (whatever you think of it.) Thais respond to flattery.

Chang Somchai, you are very skilful. I really like your work.

The idea of using a form of address according to one's age and position in the hierarchy is not common in the West. We do use "uncle" and "aunt" for much older friends even if not related, but not as much as the Thais do. They would use the equivalent much more frequently. If they ask directions of an older stranger, it would be regarded as rude just to say *khun* (Mr, Mrs, or Miss). You will find that they will say *lung* or *pa* (uncle or aunt). That would be considered polite and correct form.

Khun pa krap. (Aunty.)
Wat tee nai krap. (Where is the temple?)
Dtrong pai, liao kwa. (Straight on then take a right.)
Kawpkhun krap, khun pa. (Thank you, aunty.)
Mai bpen rai. (That's okay.)

Respect is shown by using the word *pa* and a judicious use of *krap*. It lightens the directness of the question. The woman does not always use *ka* in reply. There is no need as she is speaking to a much younger person and the respect, difference in age, and status between them has already been established. If she were speaking to someone nearer her own age, she would use the polite form of *ka*.

From someone that does not know you, it is likely you will be called *farang*. Some Thais will use the word in a deprecating sense, but not many will. *Farang* does not have any derogatory meaning. Thais are rarely racist or rude to your face. A young child may call you *farang* as that best describes the fact that you are white and not Thai. If he knows your name, he may say "*lung* George" or "*pa* Sheila." If he does not, then you may well find yourself addressed as *"lung farang"* or *"pa farang"* as a courteous alternative.

The British have no identity cards. Nevertheless, putting, quite legally, the word "Dr" on a driving licence can occasionally help with avoiding minor traffic violations if a police officer thinks the PhD is a medical qualification. More often than not though it would have no affect at all. In Thailand, the impact would be much more pronounced. If an ID or business card is produced showing a doctorate or the word *ajarn* on it the driver will receive a smart salute and be waved on. Your position in society would have been quickly noted. Class is alive and well in this country.

Thai society is highly controlled by hierarchy and class. Everyone is higher or lower than the next person. It is firmly established in Thai families when one is born. Even a small difference in age is important. All your brothers and sisters will either be *pee* (pronounced "pea" as in the vegetable) if older than you or *nawng* if younger. In Thailand, *Nawng* Jane will invariably *wai Pee* Nit first. And *Pee* Nit will not necessarily always return the *wai* to her junior sister. The *wai* is the Thai equivalent of a handshake and is formed by putting the hands together in a prayer-like movement, the thumbs always pressed into the hands and never pointing backwards to your body.

One exception to the rule of saying *pee* to an elder is after marriage. A husband with an older wife will call her *nawng* to emphasise his status as the senior person in the marriage!

I know two twins. Despite the fact that their age difference can be measured in minutes in western terms, Thailand insists that one is referred to as *pee* and the other *nawng*.

This concept of the young respecting their elders and being somewhat subservient to them is taught from birth. It is never queried. It is a structure that works well in a society that is traditionally conservative and where people feel comfortable in knowing their place. For a Thai, life is predictable and well ordered.

The rules also change when a higher-ranking person in government or business is younger than you are. Then you say *pee* to the boss despite his being younger. Instead of using *pee*, an older subordinate employee could always use a title, such as *wanna* (boss), which might be more acceptable and make the speaker feel more at ease.

Thais mainly use the word *khun* in speaking to *farangs* because they know that the *pee* (older person) and *nawng* (younger person) concept is not fully understood in the West. They need to accept you into their culture before they are relaxed with addressing you as *pee*. It is rarely used in addressing a *farang*, though it is more likely if you are speaking in Thai and you are seen as doing things the Thai way.

The giving or receiving of respect depends more on hierarchy than on being earned. In the West, one generally has to work on being valued by others. Your position does not give you any rights of being held in high esteem as it would in Thailand.

On the Queen's birthday, also Mothers' day in Thailand, I was helping in a community project, planting trees as part of the village's celebrations. Well over half the community got together; which is typical in this country. Everyone knew me and we joked and worked alongside one another. We lunched and drank together. We were all on first name terms. No *khun*, no *farang*.

Loudspeaker systems are used extensively to communicate in Thai villages, so I was not surprised later that evening to hear the *puyaibaan*, the village headman, thanking everyone for their efforts. Then I heard my name mentioned in dispatches. "*Farang Matt*" was being singled out as the only *farang* who had helped. It was not ill mannered. It was not impolite. It was the easiest way to tell the few people who had not been at the planting, the names of those who had attended. It was probably also his clever way of getting more people to be involved in future village projects. He was also following the Thai trait of putting a positive spin on events. He was emphasising those who came and not those who did not. Thais talk of half-full bottles and not half-empty bottles.

Although there is a word for "foreigner" in Thai, *kon tangchat*, it is rarely used. *Farang* is used for a person who is white-skinned. Asians, Muslims, and Negroes are called *kon asia, khaek,* and *kon negro* respectively. Hindus and Sikhs are often mistaken as Muslims, so they are also called *khaek*. The word Negro is not pejorative in Thai. Asians may also be called by their country of origin. For example, Laos is a sovereign state and their people may be referred to as *kon lao* or *kon asia*. Many Thais can trace their origins back to that country.

We use the word *"farang,"* in *Thailand Take Two*, because it is regularly used by Thais and makes the important distinction between a white Westerner and foreigners who are not Caucasian.

Colonel Jaran: What are you doing, soldier?

Bancha: Breaking eggs so that I can make omelettes for the men, sir.

Colonel Jaran: I realise that, soldier. Even so, you are breaking them two at a time.

Bancha: That's quicker, sir.

Colonel Jaran: What if one of them is bad?

Bancha: A bad egg, sir? In the Thai army, sir?

An amusing anecdote but an unusual one. As much as they love making jokes, Thais would not normally say anything like that to a superior. They are far too conscious of a person's position and any possible loss of face or respect.

But, as we see when we meet Bancha later, after he leaves the army and returns to the building trade, he can be a rather untypical Thai.

Thais realise that by acknowledging authority everyone will consider them polite and acting properly and in accordance with society's norms. It is the natural order of things here. Pushing oneself forward or being assertive is not good form. Thais have difficulty understanding why foreigners can be so familiar. They favour a more formal relationship, particularly on first meeting. In a stratified society such as Thailand's, they feel more at ease with that.

Loyalty is a strong force in Thailand. To the King, the nation, the family, one's elders, and one's superiors in the workplace.

The Thai social order starts with His Majesty the King, a monarch most revered by his people throughout a reign that started in 1946. HM King Bhumibol Aduladej the Great is the head of state in Thailand's constitutional monarchy. His Majesty is only the seventh Thai king to be given the name Great and is first in order of precedence in the country.

The royal family and those related to the royal family follow next with those in senior government, military, and business positions behind them. Although not part of the same power network; doctors, lawyers, academics and teachers are well regarded and can exercise some influence over others. Power is tolerated but not challenged in Thailand.

It is rarer in Thailand than in the West for people to move up or down the social ladder. Your position is determined by your status at birth, your wealth or that of your family, and whom you know.

Once in a job, particularly in government or the military, the employee can feel secure. It is difficult for a senior person to be made redundant in Thailand. The *avuso* concept (a sinecure, jobs for the boys.) is prevalent, well known, and accepted. "Letting people go" is rare in Thailand.

Moving to an inactive post is the means of actually firing someone and avoids a potential argument and loss of face.

In Thailand, one's position in the social structure and the level of exposure you have to the system of patronage are major considerations when it comes to job promotion. Money and contacts can help. Promotion by merit alone would seem odd to a Thai. Knowing someone who you regard as your patron or protector is useful. It could be a senior work colleague, a powerful family friend, a government official, or your local village headman, *the puyaibaan*.

The wearing of the right school tie and dating the chairman's daughter affects job prospects as much here as in western societies. At one promotion interview in Bangkok, which lasted just a few minutes, the only question asked was "Who is your boss?"

Suda: Good morning, (Sawatdee ka.)
Interviewer: Please sit down.
Suda: Thank you, (Kawpkhun ka.)
Interviewer: Who is your boss?
Suda: Khun Manat, ka.
Interviewer: Good. I know him.

She got the job. Other interviewees, some of whom had travelled overnight at their own expense, received more taxing and relevant questioning. Nevertheless, they faced an overnight return journey with no promotion offers in their pockets.

Pulling rank and using one's influence is common and tolerated in Thailand. Lawyers and teachers will always let you know who they are. High-ranking police officers will have a nameplate showing their rank outside their private homes.

Having money, and letting the right people know it, can make life more pleasant and bring added comforts and power. It can open up opportunities for career development but does not inevitably result in a step up the social ladder. Those with old money and the right family name are firmly on the top rung of the job ladder. The nouveau riche may aspire to high positions and many achieve good jobs but they do not command the same respect as the old guard. They don't exhibit the same confident air as members of the older and powerful families seem to possess. That comes with years of breeding and sets those with new money apart from the established élite.

As well as observing these hierarchies in the military, the office, and the lecture hall, you will see it for yourself when you visit Thai villages.

The *puyaibaan*, as an elected member of the community, sorts out all minor problems that occur in day-to-day village life. In any dispute, his decisions and reasoning are usually accepted. Any challenge would be made tactfully, in a round about way, and never publicly. However, that would be unusual. In this country, one tends to appease those in authority, whether they are village elders, your superiors, or the police. The *puyaibaan's* most difficult task is to be fair and maintain a balanced mind. Because he cannot please everyone, his role demands, to be effective, that he has charisma and respect within the community.

All Thais engage in *pootwan*, sweet talk. They smile and make delicate suggestions, avoiding any conflict or loss of face. They "go round the houses" and speak indirectly. However, even that does not solve every disagreement. If a problem is not resolved at the *puyaibaan's* level, it can technically be taken up with the district office and ultimately at provincial governor level. The officers at district always go back to the headman and discuss it. A compromise may be reached or his decision will be confirmed.

It would be unusual for Thais to go to the police to obtain any legal redress. Using a mediator or the *puyaibaan*, (as a person well established in the local hierarchy) is the number one preference. But using violence and aggression to settle scores, taking the law into their own hands, is not uncommon as a last resort. It may even be accepted informally by the *puyaibaan* as the best way to solve a dispute.

Thai government is not run on federal lines. The country has one national government but keeps aware of local opinion through the network of provincial, district, and sub-district administrations, right down to the village headman. That does not, however, mean that all national laws are followed in the regions. Thais are very individualistic and feel no compunction to toe the government line or that of any power network on every occasion. Nor do they feel obligated to abide by all rules and regulations.

I had stopped at an intersection when a police officer had halted traffic in my lane. As he later called me forward, he noticed a motor cyclist was blocking our way. He signaled for him to move back but he did not do so. He went over to him and I assumed he would make him move to allow traffic to proceed. The biker just ignored him and stayed where he was. The officer came over and told me to get round him as best I could and not worry if I hit him. A conflict between the police and the motor cyclist was avoided. Both the law and its enforcer were ignored. Thai individualism won the day. I slowly maneuvered my car round him and went on my journey. I doubt a western policeman would take such a *mai bhen rai* approach.

Such an example not withstanding, Thais in the main will conform to the rules provided they accept their logic. Rarely does law and order imposed by a national government fall into that category. Rules that were learned in the family from the day of a child's birth are never in dispute. The notion of family is so strong. They participate in political demonstrations and local politics but are usually reluctant to attack the current status quo or the present structures that underpin society. It is true that the universities, here as elsewhere, have traditionally been breeding grounds for newer and more enlightened ideas.

Perhaps a little like how an English lord of the manor held sway over villagers in the last century. Thai society can appear just as feudal and some commentators consider that this attitude is linked to a fear of the select few. You are unlikely to disagree with a large landowner or businessman who can decide whether you can earn a wage or not. You do not oppose the rich movers and shakers in your community. The English saying, *the rich man in his castle, the poor man at his gate*, still has some significance in developing countries today.

Thais willingly accept this. They have a strong faith in the Buddhist idea that past karma has positioned certain people in the roles they have today. One should accept one's present station in society as a result of one's past karma. Being ambitious or striving to progress in life can be taken as over-stepping the true destiny determined by one's class. Buddhism teaches non-attachment to material things and avoidance of craving for present day riches for their own sake. Karma will yield its rewards in a future life.

There are structures of hierarchy everywhere in the world.

In the early seventies the churchwarden of a village in Essex arrived late for a church service (his prerogative of course) and made a parishioner move from the family pew traditionally reserved for the senior churchwarden to a seat further back. And there were only five people in church. Including the priest.

The churchwarden's son, who effectively inherited the position many years later, was much more liberal and down to earth. Even so, his voice was listened to more intensely at church and village meetings and he usually had his own way. The family history of being a generous benefactor to the church and his habit of pulling out a chequebook whenever a donation was proposed probably helped. Everyone noticed that he was referred to as Mr Johnson and the other churchwarden, a hard working lady of the same age, as Joan. That is a true story from the early years of the twenty-first century.

In Thailand, you can see the same deference to the élite. The great and the good are invited to take front row seats at a funeral even though they are not family members. Top officials give speeches at a wedding by virtue of their position. The rich and powerful can determine whether a factory or a new road in the village gets planning permission or not. In politics, the élite, who are mainly in the capital Bangkok, are not openly challenged by the ordinary voter. Though in the North of Thailand, where the former Thai Rak Thai and the Peuea Thai parties have strongholds, there have been challenges to the Bangkok power bases, principally because of the North's links to the Thaksin family who originated from there.

Integrating and being more at ease with Thais can be achieved by understanding and accommodating some of the Thai ways that we may find unusual and frustrating. Going along with their formal and informal rules of hierarchy is crucial. The Thais will appreciate your fitting in to their culture and you will get more out of your stay in this country; however long, however short.

A Thai does not think in a western way and his sense of station in life is overriding in all he does. He accepts his lot with a cheerfulness and relaxed attitude that is the fundamental Thai quality of *mai bpen rai*, which we look at in the next chapter.

Chapter 2

Does Mai Bpen Rai always mean Never Mind?

Give me grace to accept with serenity
  the things that cannot be changed,
  Courage to change the things
  which should be changed,
  Living one day at a time,
  Enjoying one moment at a time. (The Serenity Prayer, Reinhold Niebuhr)

You will hear the phrase *"mai bpen rai"* every day in Thailand. The glossaries in most tourist guides define the Thai expression as "never mind." There are, however, many different meanings. It is a Thai mind-set that creates a hassle-free outlook on life. Why worry or get stressed about things that you cannot control and consider not that important? That is the basis of *mai bpen rai*.

Let's look at some examples from daily life.

You bump into someone in the market and excuse yourself by saying "sorry."

The response? *Mai bpen rai krap.* That is okay. It does not matter.

You thank a passer-by for giving you directions.

The response? *Mai bpen rai krap.* This time it means something like "my pleasure" or "you're welcome." The French would say "de rien," the Germans, "bitte schön," and the Italians, "prego."

You are discussing some alterations to a building plan and the architect does not see why you want an extra shower room with access from the garden.

His response? *Mai bpen rai krap.*

A female speaker would say *mai bpen rai ka*. The use of *krap* or *ka* at the end of sentences is a polite form of speaking. It has no meaning.

You can't understand why the architect is telling you that it does not matter. It's what you want him to do and you are, after all, paying his fees.

You explain your reasoning but get no immediate commitment for change. His initial reaction is not to problem-solve. Thais dislike dealing with problems. Usually, the response is to ignore or treat as insignificant. He is looking for compromise and flexibility, or to see if you will back down. As a *farang*, you are surprised he is not addressing your concerns.

It is better to *pootwan*, sweet talk, and be patient rather than to try logic and reason. Smile and say you still think it may be a good idea. Praise the work he has already completed. You can always raise the point again if it is not done. Don't say anything that sounds like you are complaining. That approach will lead to his thinking you are trying to make him lose face. That's never a good idea, especially in front of others.

What the architect meant was that he did not consider it important enough to have been in his original planning. He will change it discretely and without losing face if that is what you really want. It is not that it does not matter to him. He values your custom. He is saying that you are making an issue out of something that he personally thought was not that essential.

A few days later, the plans will be altered and you will get the extra shower room that you requested. He won't comment further or apologise. Thais will cover up mistakes rather than suggest a solution or admit an error.

Thais feel *farangs* can be rather abrupt when speaking and are too uncompromising and formal. The Thai way is to be less direct and not so forceful in conversation. *Mai bpen rai* is more an attitude of mind related to the relaxed lifestyle than a mere set of words. It is a way of thinking that is consistent with the Thai way of life and their aversion to having to deal with arguments or quarrels. Life is for living; be happy and avoid stress. Happiness and fun (*sanuk*) are their watchwords. The word "serious" does not exist in the vocabulary of the Thai.

You book a table in your local restaurant. When you arrive, you find they have stopped serving and the kitchen staff has gone home early. Will you be angry or annoyed, or will you be Thai and say *Mai bpen rai krap?* You won't die of hunger while trying to discover another eating-house. You may even find the next one will become your favourite place for a meal. *Mai bpen rai* is about being as easy-going, calm, and patient as you can.

You will find the Thais very tolerant until they feel they can take no more. They will then smile, may well walk away, but seldom will they continue to argue with you. Only as a last resort or under provocation will they get angry.

The smile will still be there but the pent up anger will not be that clear to make out. You won't see it coming. If they get violent, there will be no warning sign. To avoid the situation, stay calm, keep your voice down, and don't come across as wanting to perpetuate the row.

Walking away may feel like surrender in the West, not standing up for your principles. We feel the need to stand our ground and explain our point of view. The Thais see that as confrontational. In Thailand, steering clear of argument is the normal way out of avoiding further quarrels. Thais don't impose on other people. The term in Thai is *greng jai* – a feeling of compassion for your fellows. It is time to politely move on. Discretion is the better part of valour.

Keeping passions bottled-up is not always a good idea but it is a Thai characteristic. In an argument, the Irish and the Italians, for example, are more likely to release their bitterness immediately and get it out of their system – many would say that doing so is healthier than keeping the anger pent up inside.

Some time ago, Goong, our cashier at the photo shop, was under a lot of pressure in her job. Staff shortages meant she was being overloaded with work, with little help or support from management. She was blamed for computer problems that were not even her responsibility. Goong did what all Thais do and tried to ignore the situation and its pressures – *mai bpen rai*, keep calm, don't let it get to you.

But it did get to her. She was admitted to a psychiatric hospital for a week. Drugs helped her recovery. Compassion and understanding from her colleagues helped more. Keeping her feelings to herself and trying to control her emotions, as all Thais do, had not been a good idea.

The store does not have what you are looking for. The sales staff may possibly ask if they can order the item for you, but are more likely to say that they do not have the item in stock and politely smile. It may be that the item is in the warehouse and it is not convenient to fetch it right now. Thai customers would smile and adopt the *mai bpen rai* attitude. They would realise the sales staff's explanation is just a white lie.

Our response should be to smile back, say *mai bpen rai krap*, and try another shop.. However disappointed we may feel, it is not a life threatening state of affairs. Let it go. Westerners have difficulty grasping this Thai view. I did when I first arrived. Even after a decade in Thailand, *mai bpen rai* can still surprise and frustrate every day.

Bureaucracy is the same the world over. Go to any government department, take all the documentation that has been requested, wait patiently in a queue, and expect to be passed from one official to another. When told you need two further photocopies of your identity card, just say *mai bpen rai* and stroll round to the photocopy shop. Showing anger or complaining will be to no avail. They consider shows of irritation a character failing. Thais don't understand why foreigners do not realise they are losing face by displaying their emotions so readily. To them, loss of face is almost a cardinal sin. To us, we may not like losing face but we move on. We forget perceived slights quickly. They do not. Adopting the same attitude as they do, and taking it as inconvenient but not that vital, is probably the better strategy. Just re-join the line. On a follow-up visit, the extra requirement may well be something entirely different anyway.

Much depends on whom you see or which government office you attend. Rules can be interpreted with great flexibility in Thailand, apparently changing from one day to the next. They believe wholeheartedly that it is a game that has to be played, so just go with the flow. Try not to let bureaucracies get to you. Aim not to take the frustrations to heart. It is a bit annoying but does it really matter? *Mai bpen rai* is your defense mechanism in Thailand as elsewhere. Thais more often than not avoid clashes and disagreements by saying *mai bpen rai* and walking away. They don't outwardly show their frustrations; they have been brought up to keep a low profile and keep emotions to themselves: they camouflage their feelings so that you do not know their inside emotions particularly if they are anti-social.

Thais do not let people get the better of them. Their motto is: *don't let the bastards grind you down.*

Thais have zero inner personal respect for petty bureaucracy. This is another nuance of *mai bpen rai*, a dislike of the "job's-worth" official who plays everything by the book and ignores common sense solutions. Inside, the Thai may be seething with anger. Outwardly, he takes the *mai bpen rai* view and accepts it because he feels it is outside his control. Contrast that with the total respect he has for family and monarchy. That matters very much to Thais.

They can be very indifferent and inconsiderate in actions that they believe to be unimportant. Motorcyclists routinely pull out of side roads without looking, seemingly unaware of the danger. This indifference is a form of *mai bpen rai*. Do they really believe that providence and not their lack of riding skills will determine the timing of any fatal accident? Unless under the influence of alcohol or drugs, motorcyclists will not usually be found at fault when police are called to a collision with a car. The logic appears to be that, with a minimum wage of 300 baht a day, the rider is unlikely to have as much money as the motorist. Q.E.D. then; it's fairer for the motorist to pay.

Watch workers cleaning a drainage canal and note how they just leave the debris on the side of the bank. *Mai bpen rai* is well established in their philosophy.

What is the point of cleaning up? The weather and the passage of time will eventually rot the waste material and compost it into the soil.

Quality assurance is a tricky job in Thailand. QA engineers have to keep a distance between themselves and the workers as they are aware of the tendency for poor workmanship or mistakes not to be taken seriously. In construction projects particularly, standards and much lower than in the West. You will find exceptions, but most craftsmen don't strive to complete jobs properly. Corners will be cut. The attitude is that it is good enough, it will probably work, and it will be okay. It doesn't matter too much. *Mai bpen rai*. QA men will, on not approving some outside paintwork, spray some prominent "X" marks on the walls to ensure the whole areas gets a second coat and not just a quick repair to a few spots. They will then walk away. They won't discuss or reason with anyone. There must be no argument and no loss of face. The workers' practices are culturally accepted but the engineers must make a stand against *mai bpen rai* to protect the customers' interests. The fact they won't openly discuss the matter with the workers but merely go to another building on the site shows their discomfort in doing something which is fundamentally "un-Thai" – criticising.

Ordinary Thais are very down-to-earth and are expert in determining whether something is essential or not. A schoolgirl, with maybe only one school uniform to her name, would not adopt a *mai bpen rai* attitude when considering whether to clean and iron her uniform each day. For her to be tidy and smart at school is important to her. Appearance and dress is of great significance to all Thais, a lesson their families instill in them from an early age. Schoolboys are equally fastidious about their uniforms even if it is mum who ends up doing the ironing.

There is a *mai bpen rai* attitude in the workplace too. Festivals can be more important than meeting a deadline. The work can always be finished tomorrow. The partying cannot possibly be postponed. The three official days of the Songkran holiday in April, marking the Thai New Year, are often extended to a week. Construction workers will take the opportunity to visit family up-country. They may decide not to return. Or, they may return a year later as if there had been no period of absence. Neither worker nor employer would be surprised. In the West, workers would not expect a new post to be made available for them if they had been absent for such a long time. A job is seen as a means of getting money for short-term needs and not a way of life. If they are able to, Thais move to new employment when they are bored. They would still keep in contact with ex-colleagues but there is no sense of group loyalty that would make them stay with a single employer.

Thailand is a labour intensive economy. The agricultural and construction sectors particularly do not rely on technology as much as we do in the West. Absences from work, however inconvenient to the employer, have to be accepted. That results in low productivity but because labour is relatively cheap the practice is accommodated.

The loyalty expected in the master / servant relationship in, for example, upper class households in Victorian Britain would be anathema to the Thai. In England, below stairs staff would serve for life and that obligation would be reciprocated by a beneficent and protective employer until the servants retired and even then they would be given some support. Thai staff work without question to comply with their positions in the class system but are not loyal to the same degree. Staying with a sole employer or company is unusual in Thailand.

Spending quality time with family is a better option than getting back to work on a building site on time. We should work to live and not live to work. The Thai work ethic includes allowing employees time off to attend family events, merit ceremonies, and to organise personal business. The worker may not always be paid but the practice is accepted and customary.

Office staff will think nothing of having a break to make garlands and decorations for an office or private party. That is considered perfectly acceptable. There is always a sensible work and leisure balance. They are not being lazy. The work will be done eventually and they will enjoy doing it as much as they got pleasure (*sanuk*) from making the party decorations. Their lack of conscientiousness is only a perception. If they believe that the job is essential they will do it. If they don't, they won't. When asked why he had left a well paid job, a Thai replied, "It was not fun anymore."

All day without water. Fortunately, I had had an early morning shower. It was beginning to get inconvenient. I wanted to water the garden, the car needed a clean, and the toilets could not be flushed. I had checked all the plumbing and all seemed well. Nearby houses evidently had a supply. I knew I had paid the monthly water bill so I should not have been cut off. I asked Dta Sompet whom I should contact to get my supply back. Then his son-in-law came over and we realised that their new gardener, who had just finished watering their garden, had inadvertently turned off the connection to my house.

I did not expect an apology and it would have been out of place for one to have been given. I just laughed. We all laughed. Instinctively I said, "mai bpen rai krap. I'll wash the car tomorrow." It was nothing to be worked up about. Adding something after the words "mai bpen rai" can lessen any embarrassment the other person may feel and shows greng jai.

Chilling out is preferable to shouting out.

While not apologising can come across as bad manners to Westerners, it has no such implication to the Thai. They will smile or say *mai bpen rai* and it is best if one takes that as their way of saying they are sorry. They will of course make recompense for any harm they have done. Just don't expect any groveling or any admission of guilt.

Keeping appointments and always being punctual is another non-essential to the Thai way of thinking. There is some common sense in that. Does it really matter if you are a few minutes or hours late? If you are catching a plane it could be essential to be on time, for other engagements a little lateness would not be a problem. You will hear the words *mai mee panha* (no problem) quite a lot in Thailand. It is second nature for Thais to make decisions on whether something is crucial or not. They do it all the time.

What is not important to a Thai may be critical to a western mind. Are we serious too often in the West? Or, as Thais would say, *farang kit mark mark* (the *farang* thinks too much.)

Do we treat too many incidents as potential hanging offences, when really we should be saying *mai bpen rai*?

If you have seen the film *Crocodile Dundee,* you will recognise that the native concept of time is similar to how a Thai considers time. The Thai belief in the transitory nature of life underpins his concept of time. The uncertainty and impermanence of existence taught in Buddhism colours his view of time being insignificant.

Walter explains to Sue, the American reporter, that she will be in capable hands with Dundee as he takes her on a few days trek into the bush to write her newspaper story. Walter will pick them up on Wednesday.

Walter to Dundee: *Till Wednesday. Cheerio.*
Dundee: *Wednesday? What's today, Walt?*
Walter: *Monday.*
Dundee: *No worries.*
Walter (to himself): *Doesn't know. Doesn't care. Lucky bastard.*

Walter uses the word "lucky" as a compliment to Dundee's relaxed attitude to life. He envies his capacity to regard time as unimportant. In Thailand you will discover that time does not rule the Thais. They are the masters; time is not their master. Thais wear watches to show status, not to be kept informed of the time of day.

No rush, no urgency. It sometimes appears that the Thais have little ambition. Talking about whether the country should consider investing in international space research, a Thai quipped, "Let the Americans do it."

Thais work very hard and pace themselves if working outdoors in the heat. In schools and universities, they study for longer hours than we do in the West. So, yes, they have some ambition. It is just that it is not always all consuming. Aspiration is tempered by doing the minimum necessary to earn enough to live on. They think about "sufficiency" – a Thai concept that suggests ensuring the population has enough to satisfy its own needs. Each village or district is encouraged to be relatively self-sufficient. The theory gained ground after the 1997 economic crisis showed the folly of an over-reliance on foreign capital inflows and striving for growth through exporting to external markets to the detriment of home consumption.

"I will come tomorrow" really means that you can expect a visit at some other time. It is unlikely to actually mean "tomorrow." You may also infer that it means "no", that he has no intention of ever coming. It is a face saving reaction. So, never believe "tomorrow" always means the day after today. It may mean, "I don't want to come. I don't want to do it." Continual procrastination is better than a negative response.

In the Thai language tomorrow is *prungnee*, although one wonders if it should ever appear in a Thai dictionary with that definition.

Perhaps planning for tomorrow is not that relevant. The present and what you are doing today is of more concern than what you may or may not do in the days and months ahead. Buddhism teaches that one cannot control or influence what happens in the future. Life is not permanent. Is there any point in planning or worrying? Thais will (sometimes) plan ahead of a business meeting, but they can never be accused of being control freaks in such situations.

These are not criticisms; they are observations. We should accept them in the same way that we should accept that being too serious over things we cannot always control is often of no benefit to us. The stress created could even harm our health.

After thinking something through carefully, Thais may consider some actions not to be that critical after all. Minor irritations and frustrations will disappear with a dose of *mai bpen rai*. Thais don't get frustrated if they have to wait for a police officer to arrive following a house break-in. It may be he can not come until tomorrow because he has to attend an official ceremony today. This is an example where it may be better for a Thai to have different rules about *mai bpen rai*. Though I doubt most Thais would ever think about changing their attitudes in order to provide a prompter service. *Mai bhen rai* would have to surrender its powerful influence first.

A family will be saddened by the death of a loved one. However, they cannot bring that person back or change the course of events. They will be realistic about it. Their love remains and they still have their memories. You see smiles at bereavements. It is the end of a life in this world but not the end of the world. Here, *mai bpen rai* does not mean, "it doesn't matter." It means that nothing can be done about it, it is outside their control. It is about taking sadness and difficulties in one's stride and moving on. It is important not to show one's feelings to others. Thais don't wear their hearts on their sleeves.

Mai bpen rai is a difficult concept with many subtle meanings. You will discover more and more of them while in Thailand. It is also the attitude of doing what you want to do, and being free to ignore rules that you think are inappropriate.

The annual slash and burn farming practice in the North causes smog and results in many hospitalisations for breathing problems. It is a good example of *mai bpen rai*. Warnings are given out annually but the regulations are never enforced. It's not seen as that necessary. The police may approach the farmer and see the ashes of a fire still smoldering in his yard, but Thai logic will argue that there is no proof of a link between the owner and the burning. Nobody saw him light the fire. Neither the police nor the farmer wants any conflict. Nothing will be done.

The response is, "Well, it only happens for a few months of the year. Not that crucial."

It is sometimes tricky to reconcile the ordinary Thai's feelings of kindness and extreme consideration towards other people with their *mai bpen rai* attitude to life. It is something they learn from their parents and is reinforced in the schoolroom. Why do they turn a blind *mai bpen rai* eye to the causal link between smog and respiratory illness one minute, and share their garden produce with you, *nam jai*, (caring and sharing), the next? Being considerate towards you while not forcing their opinions or views on you. Always careful not to let you feel they are imposing, *greng jai*.

Nam jai and *greng jai* are similar but not the same. *Nam jai* is the desire to help and share, for example by giving a money envelope at a funeral or house warming. *Greng jai* is consideration for others by not being assertive or pushy, not putting yourself in a position where you owe a debt of gratitude to another person, and not asking for any favours in return. Thai culture is about giving and not receiving. And it is done in a natural way with no immediate sense of obligation. Returning kindnesses and hospitality will happen but it won't appear as a forced or unnatural response. The Thais would probably say that it comes from the heart. In fact, the name for heart in Thai is *jai*.

Ask a Thai if he is hungry and he will say no. Bring some food to the table and ask if he would like to share with you and he will happily agree.

Thais want to be laid-back and not be so serious, but they also want to show that they care and have consideration for others. That can sometimes appear contradictory.

At a road accident, they will arrange to get the victim to a hospital, but will not be anxious or annoyed if they have to make several telephone calls to ensure an ambulance arrives. Going out of their way to help, and then seemingly taking a more casual attitude. In the West, we would be getting agitated to get things done. Here, it is *nam jai* followed closely by *mai bpen rai*.

The stories on Thai driving in *A Thailand Diary* give examples of the police stopping motorcyclists at roadside checkpoints to catch those not wearing helmets. The officer salutes. The rider smiles. A fine is levied and the motorcyclist – now wearing his safety helmet – rides on. But only around the next corner. He pulls up, takes his helmet off, puts it into the front basket, and then continues his journey.

The choice that a rider takes on whether to keep the helmet on or not depends on how important he considers safety and keeping to the law. He thinks of the relevance of *mai bpen rai* at all times. He is not worried by a further checkpoint down the road. He would just show the officer his receipt for the fine he had just paid and he would be let off. I doubt that would happen in the West.

When I asked a rider why he routinely did this, he told me that it was because Thais value their freedom to do what they want. He told me that Thailand means Land of the Free. The spelling of Thailand in Thai script suggests that the meaning is actually "land of the Thai" but many still consider Thailand translates to the land of the free. There is no harm in that.

Mai bpen rai can also mean, "don't worry about it." A driver accidentally scratches another car while reversing. If the damage is slight, the owner may say, *mai bpen rai* (don't worry, let's ignore it.) He does not want there to be any bad feeling. Nothing to get excited or worried about.

If the episode involved a *farang* or a rich Thai, he may be less inclined to say *mai bpen rai*, not wanting to miss the opportunity of extracting a little money. The well to do Thai would consider the other motorist not assuming a *mai bpen rai* stance as being a little mean and not following the usual Thai philosophy of ignoring minor problems. But he would take it on the chin and pay up in the same way that the *farang* would.

A stray dog found without a collar would be impounded by the police forces of most countries. In Thailand it seems they have a right to roam free anywhere. The Buddhist concept of not killing any animal leads to Thais allowing their pets to wander wherever they wish. They don't think it is that necessary to keep them under control. This live and let live attitude is a type of *mai bpen rai*.

It is interesting that there is little awareness of foreign affairs here. Indeed, there is little knowledge of the country's own past. History is not a subject that results in any careful examination or discussion. There is a little bit of *mai bpen rai* in this Thai attitude of not wanting to learn any history or keep up with the news. It is seen as not having a great relevance to the present day. The very word history in Thai, *ponsawadarn* means "story of the kings." Not much other history was recorded. Unless very important, many national or world events are viewed as of little significance. They don't matter. *Mai bpen rai.*

Thais are more emotional than intellectual. Which is why they smile when they see you and come across as being so friendly. You will not see many books in their homes. An ambitious thirst for knowledge is not a particular priority. It is as if it does not matter. People interest them more than books.

It is not always easy to find out what is happening outside one's immediate vicinity because such news is not regarded as a matter of concern for the locals. If they feel it has no bearing on their lives, then does it matter to them? The answer is usually *Mai bpen rai.*

Thais will talk about the traffic jams on city roads and storm drains being blocked during every rainy season. Few will get proactively involved in doing anything about them. Any form of confrontation must be avoided. Although there have been exceptions, being radical or having strong principles are not Thai attributes. It is best to take the view that if you cannot do much about it, then it does not warrant a lot of effort even to think about it.

Can it be argued that *mai bpen rai* has been taken to unacceptable extremes: significant states of affairs not being willingly challenged? Do they say *mai bpen rai* and *tura mai cha*i (it is not my concern) too often?

Making payments under the counter to obtain a service to which one is in any case entitled can sometimes be infuriating or exasperating, but most Thais accept it and say *mai bpen rai*. Being held back in one's career because you are seen as not being high enough in the hierarchy or not having the right surname seems most unfair. For most Thais, that's just life. It is perhaps with corrupt payment demands and practices such as these that the Thai should make a stand rather than adopt this outlook.

Keeping cool whatever the circumstances is probably good advice for the *farang*. Think of *mai bpen rai*. It is essentially similar to the Buddhist idea of *Upakka* taught in meditation classes, being emotionally calm whatever the intricate situation.

There is a positive and welcome side of *mai bpen rai*. It is why we should accept their arriving late for an appointment, our turning up at a restaurant that is closed, and biting one's lip when told an obvious white lie. Not raising one's voice. Not arguing assertively. Living one's life day-to-day, avoiding conflict. It must be less stressful if we have those attitudes.

And this is precisely the Thai dilemma: dealing with the acceptable and the unacceptable parts of *mai bpen rai*.

Much will depend on people's willingness to adjust their attitude to some features of *mai bpen rai* while continuing to accept its positive qualities.

The younger generation does have a more questioning outlook on some of the old ways of *mai bpen rai*. They would like to keep the better traditions, but take a more twenty-first century approach to questions such as corruption that really should no longer be taken as inescapable. But it is never easy to fight vested interests.

To accept the things that cannot be changed; to change the things which should be changed.

Chapter 3

The Thai Smile

The world always looks brighter from behind a smile

Lanna, the northern part of Thailand, is known as the land of a million rice fields (*lan* = million, *na* = rice fields). After you have read this chapter, you may feel you want to call Thailand the land of a million smiles. The Thais, and their neighbours, are often described as inscrutable because the different meanings of their smiles are not easy to understand.

In the West, a smile always indicates pleasure. In Thailand, you cannot make that assumption. The Thai smile can express many emotions, not just that the person is pleased to see you or meet with you. For example, a smile in a club or disco is not necessarily a come-on. Far from it.

Let's look at the different types of Thai smile before we visit a department store and then a bar where we will meet some Thais who will demonstrate the Thai smile in action.

The Smile Friendly is merely a polite welcoming smile and no more. Enjoying life and having *sanuk* (fun) are central to being Thai. Why be too serious? This smile says that the person is happy and contented with life.

Smiling comes naturally to Thais; they were born with smiles on their faces. If there is a choice between smiling and not smiling, they will choose smiling every time. They see no reason not to smile. In that sense, the smile is an automatic reflex. They smile whenever they are speaking to you. **The Smile Automatic**. You should not read as much into it as you would in the West.

If a Thai doesn't want to do what you ask him, he will smile automatically. It is his natural response. You may have to be less indirect or more persuasive. Be long-winded to avoid coming across as too serious or annoyed. Introduce some friendly humour into the conversation, engage in a little sweet talking *pootwan*, get him on side, and try again. This time with a smile of your own.

We all smile when we hear a good joke, and the Thais are no exception. They love double-entendres and clever wordplay. Sarcasm escapes them because of their basic polite nature and unwillingness to engage in insults. When you joke with a Thai, you will see **The Smile Humourous**. Some people, particularly young girls, will put a hand over their lower face in a show of shyness and modesty.

It is not uncommon for motorcyclists to collide on Thai roads. If there is no grave injury or damage, the riders will just get up, brush themselves off, smile, and go on their way. **The Smile *Mai Bpen Rai*.** It doesn't really matter. It is not important. The smile defuses any tension in the situation. We might not get angry in the West over a few negligible scratches, but we certainly would not be smiling.

The Thai values his freedom so much that he takes it to extremes. Appointments will often not be kept. Jobs will not be done. They want the freedom to do what they want to do. So they smile.

A police officer fines you for not wearing a seat belt. He smiles and salutes. You smile and pay up. That's not a happy smile; that's **The Smile Downhearted**. For Thais, despondency carries no sense of dejection or despair. As a Westerner, you probably would not see any point in crying over spilled milk after such an incident, but I doubt you'd be very happy about it.

The more you get to know Thais and the more you visit Thailand; the more you will notice that they come across as having enormous outward self-confidence. Thais have big egos. They have a tendency to believe they are always right (like everyone else in the world, of course). Sometimes though it can be an illusion.

An electrician told me there was no need for an earth wire because electricity is different in Thailand. And of course, he smiled **The Smile of the All-Knowing**.

This smile can come across as patronising and even a little arrogant. Thais take pride in believing that they were never colonised and forced to accept new ideas. This can make their way of thinking appear somewhat inward looking, an inability to think outside the box.

Thais will not usually give a formal apology if they do something wrong or have made a mistake. What you will get is **The Smile Apologetic**, which you should take as an apology. It is the Thai way to say, "I'm sorry," so try not to feel insulted and annoyed, as you would if someone gave you such a smile back home. Smile back. If they have made an error, discuss how it can be resolved. Stay calm, keep smiling, and avoid showing anger or raising your voice.

Thais do things slowly; they try to avoid a war of words and will search for compromises. When they make what we may consider an inexcusable gaffe, they will smile. But they won't want to talk about it and lose face.

Khun Suchart was tired and jet-lagged when he arrived at Terminal 5 at Los Angeles International. He inadvertently picked up the wrong suitcase from the carousel and started walking off with it to the customs desk.

The farang next to him called out, "Hey, you Thai. What are you doing with my suitcase? Can't you see it has my name on the tag?"

Suchart looked down and saw that, although it was the same brand and colour, it was indeed not his case.

"I don't know why you're smiling. It's not a smiling matter."

A true and characteristic example of how Thais and Westerners see smiles differently. Suchart returned the case but did not say anything. He apologised by smiling. The *farang* did all the talking. If the foreigner had not shouted, Suchart would have politely said sorry. No Thai will get into a slanging match when voices are raised.

When a Thai is self-conscious or feels a little nervous, he can use **The Smile of Embarrassment** as a way of masking his sentiments and real feelings. There will be no conversation when this smile is displayed. He may not know how best to get around the difficulty he believes he is in. He wants to show *greng jai* and avoid conflict. He needs the situation to go away. It would not be unusual for him to walk off. He may want some time to think things over. He may even change his mind; but he will not do so that quickly. He certainly won't let you know straight away as that would be a major loss of face.

To avoid embarrassment he will address the problem from a different angle. Thais may sometimes use an intermediary to mediate on their behalf. A close mutual friend may suggest a compromise or solution. Sometimes a monk or the village headman will get drawn in. In the past, many small villages had a *cao khote*, an adviser on family matters such as marriage disagreements or other personal matters. He dealt, for example, with petty thefts and land disputes. It avoided the humiliation of personal conflicts.

This way of resolving an issue can be a little trying to a *farang* who is more used to sorting out mix-ups when they occur. Thais frequently complain about how stern and impatient Westerners can be. When you encounter the smile of embarrassment, just smile, deal with it the way they do. Time is not crucial or important to a Thai. While Mexicans embrace the concept of mañana the Thai version has a sense of even less urgency.

You will see **The Smile of Misunderstanding** when a Thai has no clue what you are talking about. Smile back, repeat the question slowly, and wait for an answer. If you still don't get a reply, ask the question using similar words. Watch whether the body language changes, indicating the person now understands you. People of many nationalities will refuse to admit they don't understand the foreign language you are speaking. It is not entirely a Thai peculiarity.

When speaking with a Thai, you may observe a pause and then a smile. This is **The Smile Encouraging**, an invitation to join in the conversation. It happens a lot when one member of a group is perhaps being a little quiet. The smile means, "I am not making a threat" and is intended to win your confidence and put you at ease. Be careful, though, because scammers and confidence tricksters as well as the ordinary honest Thai, may use it. And they will use it to their advantage.

Thais smile with sympathy when they are sad or giving bad news, an almost mechanical response they are taught from a very early age so that they don't show their feelings publicly. The English have their stiff upper lip; the Thais have **The Smile of Sadness**. In *The End of a Life*, we see that smiles do not have the same connotations as in the West. No one in the family was happy that Dta Sompet had died, but that didn't stop anyone from having a smile on his face. The smiling was not disrespectful; it was compassionate.

Smiles are not easy to distinguish. I was told to watch the eyes for a clue for their true meaning. A dullness indicates the smile is not a happy one and may even be a sign of sarcasm. I have found it a useful technique in most but not all circumstances.

This comment, made by a Thai to a *farang*, was overheard at a Bangkok cremation service.

Why do you look so sad? This is a funeral. You believe he's gone to a better place, don't you?

Well, yes, I suppose I do.

Then why are you not smiling?

A different culture; a different attitude.

Being in pain does not suppress the smile. A road accident victim, bleeding profusely, will smile at the ambulance crew when they arrive. The Thai sees no reason to appear sad or unhappy, whatever the circumstances. He is thinking practically. He's on his way to hospital where he will be taken care of.

It seems contradictory, but Thais can smile when they agree with you and also when they are in disagreement. **The Smile Agreeing** and **The Smile Disagreeing** are good examples of how Thais never show their true opinions on a subject. Only the context will provide clues to determine which smile is which in this confusing situation. Thais believe in being *jai yen* (cool hearted, calm) so that disagreements result in a smile and not outward anger.

Thailand is not just the land of smiles; it is the land of not knowing what is going on in people's minds. Are they agreeing or disagreeing?

One is reminded of the classic line in *The Godfather*: "Never let people know what you are thinking."

Not telling you what is happening is a trait you will quickly notice. Thais don't like to commit themselves or take responsibility. You can try asking a question framed so that you get a non-ambiguous answer. You may be lucky, or you may just get the smile.

I'll come back to fix the washing machine.
Will you come tomorrow?
I'll come soon
Tomorrow?
Yes.
What time? In the morning?
I'll come soon.
Shall we say 10am tomorrow morning?
Big smile. He may turn up; he may not.

Sometimes the following words seem appropriate even though Pete Seeger was not singing about the Thai:

Never saying what they mean
Never meaning what they say

Being two-faced in order not to embarrass you or quarrel with you is common. Making up a completely false story or a white lie to avoid unpleasantness or disappointing you occurs regularly. Smiling, the Thai believes, is better than being completely honest. We find it odd but Thais do this to avoid disagreeing with you (*greng jai* again) and to remain your friends.

Alex was beginning to lose patience. He had been waiting for half an hour for Bancha to turn up to give a quote some electrical work he wanted done in his home. Alex rang twice and Bancha told him he was stuck in traffic in Sukhumvit Road in central Bangkok but would be along shortly. Another half an hour went by and Bancha rang to say there was a demonstration at the intersection ahead and traffic was gridlocked.

Bancha was really some 700 kilometers from Bangkok. He was visiting his parent's home to help celebrate their wedding anniversary. He just could not bring himself to say he was not coming. At first I found it hard to believe what Alex was telling me but, having heard of many similar experiences, I knew it was true.

Thais do not want to argue and are sensitive to criticism and anything considered insulting behaviour. They have been brought up to believe that harmony is to be preferred to clashing with you. Thais may just walk away. Or, you will get either a blank look or the smile of avoiding conflict.

Both mean the same: that getting into a squabble is pointless and completely unproductive. You will need to talk about something else. Avoid disagreements and clashes. This is not comfortable territory for either of you. **The Smile of Avoiding Conflict** is the device used to avoid quarrels and fights. Shouting or getting violent is very much a last resort for the Thai when a smile fails and it can occur if you try to stand your ground instead of moving on and seeking the harmony that they feel you should be aiming to achieve. The Thai will feel that, as the indirect means of avoiding conflict – with the smile – has failed, he must resort to the fist, the gun, or the knife. It is not easy for the *farang* to appreciate that this can happen quite regularly with Thais. It comes as a shock when first observed.

Although a Thai will consider making use of a "go-between" to resolve a dispute –the village headman or a monk, for example – that does not mean that he has no sense of individuality or wanting to settle matters by himself. He still has a solid motivation of self-interest and a strong ego that can surpass, when pushed to the limit, his initial instinct to avoid conflict completely and not be vengeful. It took several years for me to begin to understand that Thais have what appears at first sight to be an ambivalent way of thinking through an issue. Their mind must be fighting with the natural feeling they have to harmonise and avoid conflict and their need, which can be equally forceful, to preserve their face and ego.

As Westerners, we are not always aware when a Thai's reaction changes from smiling or walking away to calculated revenge. First, the vacant look or the smile may turn to a sterner facial expression. The change may be slight and almost imperceptible. But it could be the first warning signal you get that the situation may deteriorate. Without further talking and certainly without any argument or discussion, the Thai may walk away. But it is also possible that the next step will be a violent outburst. Other Thais present will feel compelled to join in. In the West, we would regard a fight with several people against one opponent unfair and even cowardly. Thais don't look at it like that. Such western thinking is outweighed by their conviction that loss of face must be avenged by any means if their attempts at harmonising a problem have failed. Face is a powerful force in Thailand.

For many cultural issues in this country, the *farang* needs to suspend his disbelief at many things that he sees and hears. One cannot change a way of thinking cultivated over many generations and learnt from family and peers. Nor should we ever think of doing so. Different peoples; different cultures.

Thais tend to deal with potential conflicts by avoiding them whenever possible. We describe some situations in other chapters of *Thailand Take Two*. As with most Thai concepts, they can be inter-related. Conflict avoidance has its roots in hierarchy, face, *mai bhen rai*, and a family's economic background.

Here is a summary of how Thais cope with conflict.

1. They smile. This masks their anger and frustration but is also an indication that they prefer to adopt a *mai bhen rai* attitude to conflict situations. They understand that they can rarely influence any outcome. It is easier to go with the flow. Do as the Thais have always done. They live with the problem. It is part of Buddhist teaching not to show emotions or how you really feel. Detaching yourself from worldly troubles is a Buddhist aim. In the West, we tackle problems head on and have no compunction in positively criticising authority. Our legal system is adversarial; our parliament has checks and balances by having a loyal opposition. Opposing views are actively sought in order to try to arrive at the truth. Although Thailand's justice and democratic systems are modeled on those of the West, in practice they are not applied in the same way. Even in courtrooms, smiles can replace discussions and legal argument. Certainly, lawyers do not engage in hard questioning or attacks.

2. To avoid a war of words or even a rational discussion, a Thai will often not continue a conversation. It is a national trait not to accept responsibility and to avoid making an individual decision that could be unpleasant. An employee who is bored with his job would more likely say he is taking a few days leave to visit his sick mother than actually resign. Both employer and employee know he is not coming back. Both smile.

If a non-contentious resolution is considered possible, it is usual to let the village headman or a monk intercede informally. No one then loses face. Monks may intercede with chants and holy water. Taking a matter to the district office, the provincial government, or the courts is very rare and involves loss of face. Lawyers will be keen to do deals with the other side to avoid argument in court even though you are paying them to do battle for you. Retreating with a smile or taking the law into one's own hands as a last resort is more usual. The authorities, the police, or the judges would more likely suggest arbitration and compromise in any case.

3. Sometimes a Thai will "kick the cat." As *farangs*, we may sometimes take out our frustrations on a defenseless pet to get rid of our anger. The Thai will take it one step further. In front of the person he has a dispute with, he will scold the cat, punishing it for lying to him and stealing from him. He is actually directing his venom against the person who has wronged him. He is letting him know what he really wants to tell him if culture allowed such openness face to face. This is the Thai concept of *prachut*, where one's anger is projected at another person, animal or an inanimate object. The person, animal, or object is being made the scapegoat in place of the real target for anger. It is a means of staying friends with someone by not directly chastising the person who is the real object of your displeasure. The anthropological term is projected vilification.

4. Another device that is regularly used is the "fake" excuse. Two friends accept your offer of a lift to the train station. A colleague of theirs with whom they have a dispute overhears you and asks if she can come along too. Everyone agrees but the atmosphere is a little cold. After a short time, your two friends complain of carsickness and ask if they can get out of the car. A Thai would recognise this as a phony pretext for not staying in the car. They are reproaching their colleague in the only way they know. There is no direct criticism or squabbling but they get their point across Thai style. Sometimes claiming a headache or stomach sickness may be cathartic, a solution to alleviate a fear or complex instead of bottling

up one's emotions. As Westerners, we do not perceive what has happened or whether the alleged sickness is psychosomatic or not. The game has been played so subtly and so well.

5. Everyone gossips. Thais can use that art form to release their anger and avoid direct conflict. Dreadful revenge may be planned behind closed doors and atrocious lies may be told. Seldom will anything come of these private outbursts which serve mainly to liberate their pent-up emotions. An employee may have to say, "ka, ka, ka," (yes, yes, yes) to her boss, unable within her culture to discuss or comment on an instruction given her. Gossiping with her friends when her manager is out of the office is her solution. Anonymous letters are used for the same purpose. Thais accept rather than revolt. Prior to the abolition of absolute monarchy in 1932, there were coups and protests to effect change. There was rioting and bloodshed but not at the level seen in the American and French revolutions. The transition was more restrained. Even today, the political uncertainty and conflict in the country is not explicitly transparent in daily life. It is very much business as usual with no one rocking the boat. Individual political parties will forcefully state their case but people accept that change will come slowly and immediate conflict avoided. It is the Thai way.

6. When all else fails, indirect methods do not work, and a clash becomes inevitable, a Thai may resort to the bullet or the knife. Such cases of violence are more prevalent here than in the West. The Thai media, with no English readership to worry about and with no concerns about the repercussions on tourism, routinely report the gory details of fierce squabbles in the community. Murder is not uncommon though a warning signal of damaging your garden crops or killing a dog are typical first warnings. All will be the subject of neighbourhood gossip with the locals avidly studying the photos that the police have taken in staging reconstructions of crimes they say have been committed by those they believe are the culprits.

In the chapter, *How do Thais see Foreigners*, we see how Thais deal with political conflict and the threats of possible coups d'état.

It must be emphasised that extreme measures are very much last options. Thais believe that the application of the law of karma in the next life will take care of wrongdoing. Stressful conflict or revenge has little place in their daily lives. Smiling is better.

You go into the department store and every member of staff smiles at you as you walk along the aisles. The smile friendly. A young girl is sitting at a demonstration counter for a new promotional brand of coffee. She is bored because she doesn't have a customer to serve or chat with. But she's smiling the smile automatic. You go over to taste the coffee and make a joke, interchanging *aroi dee* (tasty, delicious) with *aree doi*. This has no meaning at all, which is why it is funny to a Thai.

This play on words brings out a broad smile as she realises that a *farang* is lightening the monotony with a popular joke. She is still smiling, but the smile has changed from the smile automatic to the smile humourous. The coffee is actually no better than any other brand, but of course, you don't say so. She asks if you want to buy some, you politely decline. She responds by saying, "*mai bpen rai ka.*" She had hoped to make a sale, but is not uptight about not having done so. She smiles the obligatory smile *mai bpen rai*. Three different smiles in as many minutes.

A young trainee is having a hard time stacking some cans of fruit. He is trying to make a decorative pyramid display, but the cans keep falling down. His manager doesn't raise his voice or get angry but he is disappointed with the trainee's efforts and the young lad knows it. His pyramid is never going to stand up. He shows the smile downhearted while listening to the manager's comments.

It isn't that the trainee is afraid of his manager. His smile shows respect and acceptance, not terror. He knows his place in the social structure and is aware of his position in the company. Western psychologists have suggested that the Thais live in fear and are therefore subservient. Smiling because they sometimes have to accept a situation and have to observe the rules of hierarchy reflects the power of these two cultural influences, not fear.

The manager smiles and remembers his days as a new boy when he made a mess of the simplest of tasks. He gives the all-knowing smile.

Never be too serious or critical in Thailand; try to react in a Thai way whenever possible.

You walk past a *farang* who is arguing with a sales assistant because his bread toaster has blown a fuse for the third time and he is fed up with having to keep coming back to the store. She smiles and arranges yet another replacement. But the *farang* interprets her smile apologetic as being facetious and rude. Why isn't she taking this seriously and acknowledging the trouble all this is causing him?

He keeps arguing with her; she does not stop smiling. The more she smiles; the more irritated he gets. His voice, from a Thai perspective, is unacceptably and unnecessarily loud. The customer perceives the encounter as ongoing rudeness. She believes she has done all she can by offering a replacement.

Her Thai upbringing is seeing things differently from the Westerner. She is trying to avoid argument and unpleasantness, trying to deflate the difficult encounter by smiling. She sees nothing contradictory about her behaviour. Her smile turns from the smile apologetic to the smile of embarrassment.

She wonders why this *farang* is getting so upset and *jai rawn* (hot-tempered). Why is he being so unreasonable and angry? Why can't he be like a Thai? Does he not realise he is losing face?

Everyone is staring at the Westerner now. He just doesn't realise that all the commotion he is causing is getting him nowhere. Perhaps he should learn to read the smiles and the body language, and to understand the Thai way of thinking on everyday matters.

The assistant has offered a further replacement. No criminal offence has been committed. Why is he being so solemn and stern? She cannot understand why he is getting hot under the collar over something that a Thai would see as of little consequence. She has never seen customers make such a fuss over the quality of goods. It is a common practice. Thais know goods can be faulty and may need to be changed several times. It doesn't matter, *mai bpen rai* yet again.

Farangs have greater expectations of goods being fit for purpose than Thais and there is little redress for poor quality in Thailand. To some extent, the stores know this. Although in this case, the assistant was trying to be helpful.

You walk further along the aisle, realising that you need to buy a spirit level. The supervisor speaks good English, but although he smiles and says he understands, you're not making any progress with him. He has no idea what the English word "spirit level" means and you cannot recollect the Thai word.

It would be easy if you could point to some on the shelves but you are out of luck. You cannot see any and you are at a loss how to describe what you want. Now you are both smiling the smile of misunderstanding. You may as well smile; not smiling won't help. You are beginning to understand Thai smiles.

No coffee. No spirit level. You are not having a good day, are you? It's time for a cold beer. Half a dozen locals are gathered around their favourite watering hole, and they smile when you pull up a stool and join them. Their English isn't any better than your Thai. There are pauses in the conversation while you both try to find the word you want in each other's language. It does not seem to matter. They smile the smile of encouragement in your direction, willing you to join in their repartee and banter anyway. You say how hot the weather is today. Not an earth-shattering observation but everyone is happy and enjoying the beer and the company.

You catch only a few words of what they are saying, but you understand that they are talking about a friend who has been diagnosed with terminal cancer. Everybody hopes he will get better or at least be more comfortable in the months ahead. Their smiles of sadness are not uncaring or disrespectful. Your bar mates are looking on the bright side, when more medication and care from family and community will make his last days as pain-free as possible. His being with friends at home is seen as something to smile and be happy about.

They change the subject to what all keen bar-goers are good at, putting the world to rights. Whether it's how they would deal with the traffic jams in Bangkok or how flood control needs to be more effective, everyone has an opinion. Everyone has something to say. Some agree; some disagree. No one stops smiling. The smiles of agreeing and the smiles of disagreement merge seamlessly, very different from the way arguments can get heated or serious in the West.

Thais can of course disagree strongly and become violent, but the issue has to be exceptionally important. Compromise is always the first option.

One of your drinking partners talks of a boundary dispute he has with a neighbour. He is not uptight about a few metres of land, but his neighbour's longan trees are towering over his garden and getting dangerously near his house. He has tried *pootwan*, sweet talk. He has tried compromising by suggesting the neighbour prune back only the larger branches. He says he calmly walked away, knowing that getting angry would not have helped. He'll go to the village headman and something will be sorted out.

I am sure readers will have guessed that when he walked away he was smiling. The smile of avoiding conflict. It is a difficult one for us to grasp. The Thai smile is not a western smile but it is still true that:

The world always looks brighter from behind a smile.

Chapter 4

Face

I pulled open the drawer and asked the carpenter who had made it if it was finished. After Bancha said that he had, I moved it slightly to show that the mortice and tenon joints were not firm. The sides of the drawer could be moved backwards and forwards.

He said he would take it away for repair – which took a week. I did not criticise. Bancha did not lose face. It would have been pointless to start an argument on bad workmanship. That would not be the Thai approach.

On another occasion, when workers were fixing an earth to the washing machine, they had grounded the appliance by taking a wire from the frame of the machine to a three-centimeter long screw put into the washroom floor.

Sakdaa, the owner of the property that I was renting, did not raise his voice nor speak bluntly or too directly. He was keeping *jai yen*, a cool heart. He calmly asked if they could make the earth by using a standard metal rod inserted into the ground outside the building as he thought that was a better way. The owner was Thai and knew how to *pootwan* (sweet talk) and to appear to be making a hint or suggestion rather than telling them what to do. His indirect speaking avoided his being seen as confrontational or complaining. The earth rod was quickly fixed in the correct position in the soil. If the job had not been done properly, the owner would have simply withheld payment and then talked further. As *farangs,* we tend to respond differently, with western abruptness and frankness.

In this scenario, Sakdaa was not taking advantage of his status in society. Although the workers did not know it, he was a retired army officer and active on the local council. Other Thais in that position might have delighted in showing off their relative power in the hierarchy, not wanting to appear weak or lacking confidence in their own place in the community. Sakdaa allowed the workers not to lose face and did not need to show off to do it.

There was no apology from the men for trying to get away with a short cut; the owner accepted that it was usual to try to cut corners. There were smiles all round. We would get frustrated when we see this happening. Thais avoid the aggravation by regularly visiting the building site where the work is taking place, at least once a day.

Employees will accept what they have to do if told by someone higher up the social scale. In fact, you will hear Thais say, "I ordered him to do it" rather than use the words "asked" or "requested." The workers would not think the choice of word unusual or rude. They may have been ordered to do something but they had not been criticised in front of anyone and they had not been shouted at. They were not losing face. That they would not have accepted.

Although money will influence Thais and may get you what you want, *farangs* are not perceived to be in any obvious social order. They truly do not know where we fit into their hierarchy. We are either here as tourists spending money before returning home or expats on renewable annual visas. In either case, we are not totally regarded as members of Thai society and are not seen as being in any social structure with which they are familiar. That, and our misunderstanding of some aspects of their culture, can make Thais a little wary of us.

The best advice is to ensure that, however well intended, comments can never be interpreted as personal criticisms or as insulting. Thais tend not to get too involved in the affairs of others if they can see the potential for a personality clash that would lead to a loss of face. They want to steer clear of any revenge that might follow, preferring to be open-minded and going their own way.

On the road, shouting at a motorist whose driving has annoyed you will achieve nothing. He will lose face and you will be seen as not being tolerant and not having a *mai bpen rai* outlook on other people's minor peccadilloes. Sticking a finger up at him could well elicit a far more dangerous reaction. There have been cases of Thais and *farangs* being shot dead following such incidents. Possession of firearms is not uncommon here. If you watch carefully, you will observe motorists winding up their windows whenever they are stationary in traffic.

A Thai who loses face believes he is losing self-respect and feels challenged. He will feel even more hurt and wounded if it is done in front of others. Any sense that you are being critical of him will be taken as a degrading attack. He may smile or walk away, but the damage will already have been done.

You may not grasp immediately how angry he has become inside. The Thai generally doesn't show his feelings. The majority of Thais are Buddhists and their religion teaches that one tries to detach oneself from feelings and emotions and not take awkward situations personally. The body language or the type of smile may show how a Thai really feels. The smile is commonly used as a safety valve when a Thai feels angry or upset.

If you have an issue with a Thai, you need to deal with it calmly and softly on a one to one basis. What you take to be merely commenting or expressing a point of view may come across as a war of words. The situation could then get vindictive, even violent, especially if others are present. Loss of face can become precariously unsafe.

Losing face means being humiliated. It is damaging to one's good name and feeling of self-worth. Thais, as well as many other eastern peoples, find this impossible to allow. No one, of any nationality, likes to be made to look foolish, incompetent, or wrong. If you inadvertently do that to someone in the West, you can apologise or explain your standpoint more clearly. That will not work with the Thai.

It is better not to get into that predicament in the first place. Thais do not like being boxed into a corner. Allow them to come away gracefully from a disagreement. Say sorry and smile. Look at it more from the other person's perspective. Otherwise, walk away. It is what a Thai would do to avoid further clashes. Discuss the matter another time using a different approach to smooth over the difficulty.

Thais are easily affronted and are completely unforgiving when it comes to loss of face. Preserving face is a feature that is non-negotiable in their eyes. They will not easily forget any lapses from it. In the West, losing face can result in one of two reactions. Either you will feel snubbed and want to get your own back; or, you will take it on the chin and rise above the snub or insult. A sensible and practical attitude may win through. Later you will probably think nothing of the incident. Not so with the Thai.

Although not usually taking life too seriously, the Thai does not treat loss of face in such a *mai bpen rai* way. Not under any circumstances. You see a smile, but he is burning with anger and disbelief inside at being made to lose face.

In Thailand you gain face and respect by helping others, by being seen to associate with the élite in your community, by being considerate of the faults and mistakes of others, by having and displaying power, by showing your wealth and position, and by keeping to the unwritten laws of hierarchy.

Thais expect that of their compatriots. It is normal practice to be active socially in the community and to help others. Not to do so would be to lose face, but that seldom happens. All Thais know instinctively and automatically how to avoid such situations. Not having *greng jai* (compassion for your fellows) and not using the right terms of address when speaking to your elders or superiors are faults that no Thai would commit.

What *farangs* do and say will signal to a Thai whether they really understand Thai culture or not. They will note if you are insensitive to their need to keep face. They will observe if you are taking life too seriously or not taking up a *mai bpen rai* attitude. It will determine how the Thais think of you. They scrutinise their fellow compatriots in the same way.

Face is lost by talking loudly, not helping your family when you could do so, and by being in a temper. To persist in arguing or reasoning your way out of a dilemma is not the right solution. Displaying anger and shouting indicates a weak personality to a Thai. They see it as a character failing.

Generalisations are not always helpful but if one were asked to sum up the Thai character the words: status conscious, pragmatic, self-reliant, independent, fun loving, and living for today would spring to mind. You may see these characteristics as you read through other chapters.

For a young lady, being jilted after her fiancé has been introduced to the family results in loss of face for her. You will not be forgiven and your position in the locality may get uncomfortable and frosty. The Thai girl was indicating to friends and family that you were much more than just an acquaintance, you were to become her permanent partner. The family often sanctions premarital sex if an engagement is announced in this manner and if a small deposit of the dowry is paid to lessen the wrath of the village spirits in the spirit houses. If you had felt that the relationship was a more casual one, it would have been better to decline the invitation to meet the family. She misinterpreted the vibes you were sending out. You misinterpreted the significance of meeting family. A Thai man would not make such a mistake. He knows the rules.

Some *farangs* in that position have found it better to move out. The community will never accept them. The clear lesson is for both the *farang* and the Thai to understand each other's culture. Not easy.

The Thais themselves are sensitive about the clothes they wear. A *farang* going shirtless or not wearing clothing appropriate for the occasion will lose face if he does not follow the dress codes of the locals. It is not just in temples that it is wide of the mark and disrespectful to wear short and revealing clothes. Taking note of what others wear and how they behave is a sensible idea in any foreign country. It is practically mandatory in Thailand. Thais instantly and continuously size you up.

Particularly in the larger cities and with the younger generation, it is no longer unacceptable to hold hands in public. In smaller towns in the countryside that would still be considered a face losing situation. You may notice that it is just not done in polite Thai society. It is not correct form. It is perfectly okay though for same sex couples to hold hands as it shows camaraderie and friendship. Men holding hands is not necessarily a sign of homosexuality in Thailand. Although not openly encouraged in such a conservative country, it is certainly tolerated and carries no stigma. Much like Frenchmen will make la bise (a kiss to the side of the cheek but without the kissing sound) to close male family members and friends. Solomon Islanders do much the same. It owes its origin to the western idea of indicating friendship by extending the right hand in a handshake to prove no sword is being carried.

Do you remember me?

Even if the person does not remember you, it is likely he or she will smile and say, "yes, of course I do." There must be no loss of face. The smile does not mean you have been recognised. It is the smile automatic. Just smile back.

Try to avoid asking rhetorical questions. A Thai will usually give the answer that he thinks you require. It is not easy, but phrasing a question so that it requires only a yes or no answer occasionally works. It suggests you genuinely want the truth. You may need to persevere or rephrase your question a few times to get a result.

It's not going to rain this evening, is it?
If you're lighting a barbeque, the answer will be "no."

If you are hopeful of some rain so that you don't have to water the garden, the answer will be "yes.' The Thai has calculated the answer he knows you want. He doesn't want to lose face by telling you something you won't appreciate.

The difficulty does not only occur in Thailand. Margaret Mead, in completing her doctoral thesis *Coming of Age in Samoa*, did not realise that her interviewees were giving her the answers that would support her point that Samoan teenagers were very different from their western counterparts. She fell into the trap of asking questions in a way that made it clear what answers she wanted. The Samoans wanted to please her so did not give her the accurate responses she was seeking. She was thinking with her academic and western hat on. They were concerned at not losing face and told her what they thought she wanted to know to support her thesis.

It was only decades later that researchers realised that Samoan teenagers were not so dissimilar from their western opposite numbers after all. They had similar sex drives and attitudes.

Teachers and university professors must never lose face. Students will not put them in a position where that could happen. They know their position in the hierarchy means that they can't ask awkward questions and put their teacher on the spot.

Students may hold radical views and have strong ideas on some aspects of Thai life but they would be careful how and to whom they were expressed. What they say amongst themselves may be quite unlike what they feel they can relay to their elders or teachers. It is never wise to assume that what a Thai tells you is what he really believes. Rarely will you learn his true opinions on a subject.

Thais are careful when speaking to their bosses or elders. They will bite their tongues rather than say what they truly believe. Face, again.

The Thai love of compromise and finding a "middle way" is actually a Buddhist theory to resolve disputes, provided of course that no loss of face is involved.

Can you direct me to the nearest gas filling station?
Go straight on and turn left at the traffic lights.

You drive on and get hopelessly lost. No filling station in sight. You may feel that is hardly considerate of the pedestrian of whom you made the enquiry. His response was purely to save face. He could not admit that he did not know where you could fill up your tank.

The dish you ordered in the restaurant is a little cold for your tastes. Instead of saying, "I can't possible eat that. It's too cold. It should have been served hot," deal with it the Thai way so that the chef and the staff do not lose face.

This looks good. My friends said I would like this restaurant. The chef certainly knows how to use herbs and spices to give the dish a distinctive flavour. Please give him my compliments.

It's just a little cold for my taste though. I wonder if he could warm it up a little.

Of course. We want you to enjoy your meal. We are more than happy to prepare it exactly how you want it.

Long-winded, but polite and no one loses face.

In summary:

* don't criticise Thais and their country: they are without exception patriotic and nationalistic.
* don't shout or raise your voice when speaking.
* don't be annoyed at not getting an apology: the Thai smile should be sufficient.
* don't dress or act in a way that Thais would find insulting or discourteous.

The Thai notion of face is difficult for Westerners to grasp. I still don't always get it absolutely right.

The tolerant Thai can accept most things but will never tolerate loss of face.

Chapter 5

Family and Community

Thai life revolves around the family and the community in a way that can be surprising for Westerners. The Thai tries to find as many ways as possible to bond with others. It is key to their philosophy of life to get on with family, community, and their fellow countrymen. Patriotism and love of the present king are two further forces that unite the Thais.

They are a social and gregarious people who thrive on contact with others, hating the solitary life. Not only the immediate family but also second cousins and aunts several times removed often routinely live together or in close proximity to one another.

Anti-social thoughts are suppressed to preserve community harmony. Klausner has referred to that environment as being "socially placid." Thais do not outwardly react to delinquent acts in the community. They are dealt with by gossiping and dropping hints to the right people. It is always an indirect approach. Directness is suppressed. "Why? Because, living in close proximity to one another, life would be impossible if basic ground rules to avoid conflict were not enforced within the group. As Klausner has said, peer and family pressure will limit the excesses of any delinquency.

So, Weelai is not typical. She has more *farang* friends than Thai and has always lived in the house in Bangkok where she was born over 70 years ago. Weelai is a retired political science *ajarn* (professor) from one of Bangkok's top universities and has never married. She has always lived alone and devoted herself to her students. When time afforded, she enjoyed her twin hobbies of gardening and collecting books on ceramics. They are mostly written in English and French, languages in which she is completely fluent.

A confirmed monarchist, Ajarn Weelai's profound love for her king is no different from that of any other Thai. All over the country, we see the king's portrait on the streets and in homes and public places. Everyone who has visited Thailand will have noticed that Thais have a deep respect for King Rama IX, always referring to him as *Nai Luang*, a term of great respect, and always saying "my king" or "our king" in conversation. I have never heard a Thai say "the king" and that is very revealing of their personal feelings towards the world's longest serving monarch. Most Thais have only known one king. King Bhumibol Adulyadej, Rama IX, has reigned since 1946. You may notice that, in this country, allegiance is to an individual and not an organisation. If you respect your boss, you will put in that extra effort to help him out with a report to his superiors. You do it for him not the company. The Thais think of their king in this personal way too.

Weelai could hold her own in any political discussion and had extensive knowledge of the systems of government in both democratic and non-democratic countries. That alone made her untypical. Most Thais have little knowledge of their history and feel ill at ease when debating even the least contentious of topics. They are happier chatting and exchanging everyday gossip with their friends and neighbours.

I first met Weelai when she was on a panel debating the American political system. Her understanding of how the senate and congress worked, her insight into the rôles of lobbyists and pressure groups, and her comprehension of how presidential elections were lost or won was remarkable. Although argument is normally anathema to the Thai, she gained great respect through her discussions on international forums, putting forward alternative views.

Her familiarity with western ways was not only obvious in her lectures on other political systems but also became apparent when discussing or explaining certain concepts that are generally regarded differently in Thai and western societies. She understood the Westerner and appreciated the cultural clashes that could occur. Her opinions on how Thais and *farangs* could find solutions to these frustrations were always well thought out and explained.

She tried to encourage the *farang* to talk less loudly and not be so assertive or "pushy" while explaining to her fellow Thais that giving honest direct answers to *farangs* is what they expect. She quoted Margaret Mead's experience where the Samoans gave the anthropologist the answers they thought would impress her rather than the correct facts she needed for her research. Weelai put in plain words that foreigners want the truth and don't mind if it sometimes hurts.

Scores of Westerners went to her with their disappointments and frustrations. She became a sort of "agony aunt" for expats in the area where she lived.

Even after her retirement, she was referred to as Ajarn Wee or Ajarn Weelai. Closer Thai friends would call her Pee Wee. (*Pee* being the respectful word for an elder.) As a *farang*, I always called Weelai, Ajarn Weelai. The shortened form that her Thai colleagues used would not have sounded right coming from a *farang* and, anyway, I could never stop myself from thinking what the words "pee" and "wee" would conjure up to an English listener.

There was always a sense of aloofness around her. Her knowledge and intellect made some Thais rather jealous of her. It's not easy to spot, but if you are watchful in your travels, you will recognise this Thai characteristic. To be fair, there is a little of this Thai jealousy instinct to be found within the expat population. A vociferous minority that recognises that they have more money than the average Thai but are resentful that they are not accepted into their social circles.

Money talks in some situations in Thailand. But it does not count for much when the Thais sense a sort of colonial attitude from the foreigner. Their excessive spending is seen as showing off and does not guarantee them entry into Thai life. Foreigners with this attitude often spend a great deal of their time in *moobaans* where there are a large number of foreign residents. In a way, they create their own ghettoes away from the real Thai communities. Thais don't regard it as any of their business but they fail to understand why *farangs* do not seem to want to fit in to the communities in which they live.

Another foreign group is made up of those who, through no fault of their own, have fallen on hard times, losing their money to scammers and fraudsters. Not all these crooks are Thai. A significant number of foreign businessmen play on their naivety and take advantage of a captive market of people who speak little Thai and become vulnerable victims to those they believe can be trusted because they are western. Pattaya and Phuket particularly have this reputation.

The Thais are somewhat jealous of foreigners because we are perceived, often wrongly, as being richer than they are. Some can be envious and want to emulate us. The hi-society people want the same as Westerners and can be seen flaunting their Rolex watches and Prada bags (copies or not.) Foreigners are charged higher prices than the locals in the tourist spots of most countries. In Thailand, it applies to both visitors and expats. It has taken hold partly because of this intrinsic jealousy that the Thai has for the wealth of others. The ever present smile camouflages the resentment and xenophobia some Thais feel towards Westerners.

Thailand is very family oriented. Members stay close throughout their lives. It is a people conscious society. A Thai family sees itself as part of the local community and ready to help others in the neighbourhood. Whether that is money, food, or rallying round when needed. *Nam jai*, giving and receiving of gifts and favours, is an instinctive part of Thai life. "*Nam*" means water and it is this idea of a "freely flowing" substance coming from the heart (*jai*) that is the origin of the expression *nam jai*.

It is a money-conscious society because money is a means of gaining esteem and prestige in Thailand. It can be employed to show off or it can be used to indicate where you stand in the community.

It is the resource that allows much reciprocal giving. The rich will give donations to local and national *wats* as well as sponsoring local amenities. Even those on low wages make donations to the *wat* and local projects. It is expected that they do so and Thais are happy to contribute to their community. It is a habitual response. A record is made of all donations – money is not given anonymously as in the West – and usually the list is read out over the local loudspeaker system later in the day. Ajarn Weelai, 1000 baht; Khun Goong, 50 baht; Chang Bancha, 100 baht.

It would be unthinkable not to give 40 or 100 baht if a colleague in your office, or a member of his family, died. From what I have witnessed, it is an unconscious response rather than giving in to any peer pressure.

Low paid workers, as a rule of thumb, budget on the basis of one third for food, one-third for accommodation, and one third for petrol for travelling to and from work. 40 baht per meal spent at a stall on the side of the road three times a day; renting a one room bed-sit with a squat toilet; and petrol for the motorbike which is on hire purchase or on loan from the family. Borrowing money from friends or family to make ends meet towards the end of the month is not unusual. In periods of austerity in the West such "payday" loans have become common place. In Thailand, it has always been a popular means of getting by until the next payday.

Getting to know the ordinary Thai will give you a good insight into Thai life and probably change some of your perceptions of Thailand. You will be taking a *second take* on the culture and life style. Talking to Thais, you will learn that for most families their parents and grand parents were from a poor background. They are therefore acutely aware of the need to have money for survival. They prefer cash transactions, cash in the hand now, than using cheques. Saving for the future is not a priority. Buddhism teaches that life is not permanent and, quite possibly, that partly accounts for this very typical Thai attitude of not worrying about tomorrow. Family and friends will always be there to help if needed.

You will find yourself being introduced to aunts, uncles, cousins, and nieces, when in fact they are just friends, close enough to be regarded as family. In time, you may find Thais beginning to accept you. They will start using your first name instead of *farang* or calling you *lung* or *pa* out of respect. It will depend on how far you have absorbed the culture and way of life of the ordinary Thai. Although they will never totally accept you – their Thainess and passionate patriotism will prevent that – the relationship will be warmer. Normally, you will have to make the first move.

We do not have that same extended family concept in the West. It is, however, interesting that we now see this in South Africa where fellow whites look after whites who have fallen on bad times. They treat them as if they are one of the family. Thailand has always had that concern for others.

The Thai will always put family before business. In the workplace, there would be no problem in attending to family matters ahead of achieving a business deadline. During the Thai New Year, it is perfectly acceptable for staff to take a few extra days off to visit relatives. Management do not normally give it a second thought. However, an architect who also owned a building firm once confided in me that it played havoc with his building schedules and that he always had headaches about missed deadlines and penalty clauses being imposed against him.

Many activities are centred on the family unit. Weddings, funerals, the arrival of a new baby, a daughter's graduation, a job promotion, a house warming. Families will get together whenever they can and keep in contact. They will turn such opportunities for contact into fun events. Even at political rallies and demonstrations you will see singing and dancing. A chance for some sanuk perhaps being more important than the political issue at stake. If you were witnessing such rallies yourself you would definitely be forgiven for thinking that. The media of course would put a more sensationalist spin on events, emphasising the violence, confusion, and crowd anger.

Cell phones are widely used to communicate with one another. Your boss won't raise an eyebrow if you're taking a short call from a relative or friend during a meeting or an extended call when you're at your desk. It can come as a culture shock to newly arrived expat workers.

A woman has a stronger bond to her family than to her husband or partner. Her bloodline is more important and relevant to her. Female liberation, women's lib, is not strong in Thailand. Her duty is to her parents and to the family in which she was brought up. A husband comes second; you marry the family not the bride in Thailand. It is the man who is joining the girl's family and not the other way round.

In *How do Thais see Foreigners*, we meet Khun Somrak and hear her commenting on her husband:

Why can't he understand that my mum and dad supported and cared for me without question as I was growing up.

As a member of the family, he must now help me look after them.

I say 'must' but I really mean "want to" It is my duty. That is what I was brought up to believe.

Somrak wants her *farang* husband to consider himself part of her family. He will never be fully accepted, he is not a blood relative or a nationalised Thai, but she wants him involved with her family.

There are many similarities between Thai lifestyle and that of China and other parts of the Far East. The burden of who looks after the family is not, however, one of them. In China, it is the son who has responsibility for his aged parents when they grow old. The "one child family" rule which effectively encouraged the abortion, abandonment or non-registration of female babies led to couples waiting until they had their first male child before deciding to have no more children. A male heir was considered that important.

Providing for one's relatives can sometimes involve a girl moving from home to one of the larger cities. She will then typically send a regular and relatively high part of her earnings back to her parents. Mostly the work will be legitimate but it can be much less savoury.

Prostitution does not have the same stigma in Thailand as elsewhere. To save face the work may be described as being in the hospitality industry or working as a cashier in a bar. The truth is understood but not mentioned. What is key is that the daughter is dutifully providing for family.

Relatives, particularly the elderly, will live on a single plot of land with the rest of the family. Newly weds will normally have a house of their own within the compound or very close by.

Despite being independent and wanting their own way, Thais have a passion for doing things together. Community functions and religious festivals at the *wat* are the common socialising grounds. A funeral will attract most members of a community whether close friends or not.

A Thai's relationships are very wide-ranging. In *The End of a Life*, we see that paying one's last respects is a duty that Thais willingly engage in. It is not so much an obligation as a natural cultural response to living in the community.

Getting on with people is preferred to not getting into disputes with them. Thais believe that it is always better to create bonds of friendship and gain useful networking contacts. Whom you know can be useful in this country.

Earlier, we heard an interviewer ask Suda:

Interviewer: Who is your boss?

Suda: Khun Manat, ka.

Interviewer: Good. I know him.

That was the only question she was asked. She got the job.

Annoy someone in Thailand and you make an enemy of his friends too; befriend him and you may well be invited into his social circle, his *phak puak*. You will enjoy life more if you participate in neighbourhood events with the locals themselves. Your experiences will be very different from those you may enjoy in a formal expats club, by only participating in expat events, or living in a predominantly foreign-dominated *moobaan* (housing estate). You will feel more a part of Thailand.

Thais are outgoing and live in groups. They could never survive on a deserted island. They need people around them. A Thai would never say, "I need my personal space."

Even Ajarn Weelai, who lived alone and immersed herself in her hobbies, enthusiastically engages in community activities organised by the *wat* or other local groups. She would never miss a religious festival.

In some provinces, it is traditional at parties for relatives, friends, work colleagues, and neighbours to give an envelope containing money to the host. The envelopes are attached to a decorated pole that is taken in procession to the local *wat*. Although the gifts are given to the host as gratitude for his hospitality (in western eyes), Thais regard it as a show of merit (*tambon* in Thai) on the part of the guests. Buddhists think of merit as being achieved by good deeds, so by giving a gift to the host you are making merit for yourself and improving your individual karma. At funerals, any merit you gain is transferred to the deceased.

Similarly, at most *tambonbaans* (house-warmings) a sealed envelope containing some money will be handed to the homeowners during the monks' ceremony of blessing. This gives the donor merit while cash is always welcome when you move into a new home. The owners will give their own cash envelopes to the monks that are present as a token of their own merit. This merit ceremony does not always take place when the new house is bought. If funds are short, it will be postponed, perhaps for a year, until money for a decent party is available. Wedding parties can similarly be delayed for this reason. Thais like occasions with *sanuk* and will wait to make sure everyone will have a good time.

Thais pop in to see friends occasionally but arranging a soirée or dinner party at home, that is then reciprocated at a future date, is not the norm. If you turn up to see someone, food will be offered but guests usually politely decline. This is the concept of *greng jai*, not imposing oneself on others. If a more formal dinner with friends is contemplated then the usual choice is to meet at a restaurant. If a Thai has *farang* friends, it may be that there is some embarrassment that the Thai home is not up to the standards of a more expensive foreign home. Eating at a restaurant solves the problem for the Thai. As a rule, the senior person, considered to be the richest, picks up the tab.

If the gathering is one that is informally organised within the neighbourhood then it is okay and customary to bring some contribution of food and drink. Even if just visiting someone it is usual to take a small gift of fruit or some other small gift. Caring and sharing is the established custom.

Thais prefer socialising in larger numbers and meeting with other people in the community. They are happier enjoying some *sanuk* with their neighbours. It makes for a cohesive and strong community spirit within society.

They seldom use the word colleague or acquaintance, though those words do exist in the language, preferring to use the word friend. "She's my friend" can often just mean someone who works in the same company as she does. She may only have spoken to her a few times. The use of "friend" makes bonding easier. There is a strong sense of comradeship, camaraderie, within all Thai groups. Keeping in touch with old school chums, people you worked with long ago, and university contacts comes naturally to a Thai. More so than in the West.

When Seri died at the young age of 42, twenty of her year group, who had graduated with her many years ago, travelled miles to be at her funeral. Taking an overnight train or flying up-country from Bangkok, necessitating a few days off work, did not seem out of the ordinary either to them or to their employers. A collection was made for the family and handed over by the eldest in the group. They helped the family in other ways too. They copied a photo of her in her university robes from a facebook page and framed it so that it could be carried at the head of the funeral procession.

At the cremation, they formed a circle around the coffin, draped with the university flag, and sang the college anthem. Generally, we see the Thai as rather stoical and not showing emotion. But singing this farewell to their former classmate brought a few tears to many eyes. It is normal, of course, to comfort people in that situation so that they regain their composure. And that happened here. What was different was that half an hour later everyone in the group was laughing and joking. In the West, there may be smiles and light chatter but not laughter and gaiety. I emphasise that there was no lack of respect. This is the Thai way of responding and getting over the grief they felt. A big cultural difference.

We saw, when we looked at the concept of face, the importance that a girl attaches to introducing a fiancé or boyfriend to her parents. She is in effect saying that this is her permanent partner and not a casual relationship. It is not so much getting family approval as making her family and circle of friends and acquaintances aware that the relationship is serious. In western cultures, it is often accepted that friendships can still be kept even after a relationship has ended. That can happen here but it is not usual. Certainly, divorced couples would not speak to each other anymore. They would, of course, smile and say what politeness required.

The Thai practice of a man giving a dowry (*sin sot*) to his fiancée's parents is a way of repaying the family for bringing up the daughter and to compensate for any loss of the daughter's income after marriage. It is still common in all but the poorest of families and, even on those occasions, token payments are made depending on ability to pay. Although a great show is made of presenting the money, it is often discretely given back to the bride and groom for their own use in their life together. Divorced women, widows, and those with children do not technically attract *sin sot*.

Farangs may perceive it as a form of buying the girl, a bride price. Thais do not see it like that. The literal translation of "bride price" in Thai is "mother's milk" which is a reference to a mother's caring for her infant after birth. The *sin sot* is viewed as a repayment for that motherly love. If the parents are not keen on the boyfriend, they never say so. They push the price up so that he gets the message. If the woman is that much in love, she will accept the parents decision now but probably elope and leave the family home and village later. The more you understand the Thais and Thailand; the more you appreciate that Westerners and Thais think differently about money matters.

Is he buying you?

Certainly not. My husband should be showing nam jai to my parents. A Thai would see it as his duty to be generous to my mother for loving me and feeding me when I was a baby. In Thai, we have the expression "the husband paying for mother's milk."

In the past, it was common practice in the West for the bride's family to pay a dowry to the husband. This was partly a prepayment of what the daughter would have inherited when her parents died. More importantly, it was a sum of money to ensure that the new couple would be financially secure. It was vital too that the daughter's social status should be upheld, keeping the family's position in the class structure intact.

Victorian families in England initiated arranged marriages where the basis of the union was money, power, and keeping the lady in the manner to which she had become accustomed. Class and hierarchy were being reinforced by ensuring that the couple was sufficiently well off to participate in the society in which they had been brought up. Love had little to do with it. The practice was not limited to the UK. It was common in other countries in the world, particularly those in Europe. *Sin sot* and the strong family tradition are the parallels in Thailand.

In Thai marriages today, both the parents and the couple see matrimony as a commitment. The amount of the dowry, and sometimes the marriage itself, is often negotiated, sometimes by a go-between, the *mae sue*. Thais in the community will take a dim view if a girl's parents try unreasonably to inflate the amount. If a *farang* takes good advice and knows the ground rules, he can avoid being caught by such a practice when a family has an incorrect assumption of the groom's wealth.

There is still some pressure for a girl to marry well, wealth not love being paramount. However, Thai parents are unlikely today to choose their daughter's husband. They might well have done so a few decades ago.

A Thai husband will continue to support his wife's family after the wedding has been celebrated and the dowry paid. He will be happy to do so. He would lose face if he did not. Giving is not all one-way. It is reciprocal. The family will help the new couple whenever it can. Thais have this strong sense of giving and sharing. The husband will look after his own family, following this tradition, though not to the same extent. Favours are always returned in Thailand. It is an expected part of the culture. An elder colleague in an office environment will look after a younger member of the team, even when that person may be nearing retirement age herself. The kindness will be repaid at every opportunity. The idea is called *bunkhun* in Thai.

Freshers in their first university term are assigned a "senior" who will show them the ropes. The relationship continues throughout the students' time in college. At faculty reunions the student will seek out and *wai* his "senior."

There are very few old people's homes in the country. The Thais do not feel comfortable with that alternative to looking after the elderly. It is anyway expensive for them. *Farangs* look at it differently. The Japanese too have no difficulty in accepting the retirement home idea and willingly choose Thailand as one of their favourite destinations for that purpose. There are several in the northern provinces of the country.

For the Thai, looking after the aged is a family and not a state responsibility. Paying a private institution to look after old granny is not a common choice. It may be that a private hospital or nursing home could provide good round the clock care; but the Thai would generally consider sending a relation there as avoiding family responsibilities. The custom is for family elders to stay at home and be looked after until their final days.

If anyone, old or young, is hospitalised in Thailand it is not unusual for a family member to stay overnight with the patient. It provides companionship and comfort. The hospital authorities welcome the provision of more intimate care and readily cater for the overnight stays by providing a foldaway bed and other facilities. It helps the patient to recover more quickly and has the benefit of someone being with the patient most of the time. Nurses still keep a watchful eye, of course.

You can set your watch by him. It is six o'clock. The national anthem is now striking up. Dta Sompet, who is 83 years old, is peddling his cycle the few hundred metres to his younger daughter's small village shop, as he has done without fail every evening for the last three years. He will spend the night there after the store is properly locked and bolted, leaving his wife, eldest daughter, son-in-law and grand-daughter at home.

His daughter, Khun Fai, who divorced several years ago, now lives alone. It is his routine to provide security for her. Helping within the family group is an overriding factor in his thinking. Filial duty is being unquestionably repaid. Blood is certainly thicker than water.

As everywhere else in the world, Thai families have their black sheep. Errant younger brothers can become addicted to drugs, be in constant trouble with the police, or be unable to hold down a job. As a son of the family, he is never turned away and every year he will get a birthday present from his elder sister. She receives no present from him on her birthday and none is expected. She is older and is expected to look after him.

Not all Thais have this caring *nam jai*. Not telling someone when a relative or friend has died does sadly happen. The thought of caring for others may be absent when greed or jealousy is involved. An illness or death in the family may be kept quiet so that not all the relatives will share in any eventual inheritance. I know of only two examples.

A brother refused to take his older sister to hospital claiming he could not drive because it was dark and his eyesight was not good. He went on to play a game of poker with his mates in a poorly lit bar. This stubbornness is not acceptable behaviour but some people are too thick-skinned to realise it. Thais do have a fiercely independent, perhaps even selfish and stubborn streak, sometimes. It is still regarded as unacceptable, although some may be too thick-skinned to realise it. You may notice that Thais will give an excuse such as this rather than just say they won't do something, particularly when talking to elders or parents.

Family loyalty trumps honesty most of the time. Cheating and even corruption will be covered up if a family member is implicated. It is acknowledged that you will lie to avoid getting a relative into difficulties. A mother will go to the police station with her

28-year-old son, arrested for riding a motorcycle without lights. She will be pleading his case. He will be sitting there playing games on his mobile phone.

A person's allegiance is, first and foremost, to family. It will take precedence over loyalty to the company you work for or any obligations you may have for your job. The exception is where you feel a personal loyalty to your boss as an individual. It would not be unusual to work overtime or at weekends, unpaid, to help a superior finish a task or meet a deadline. But it is a commitment to the person not the organisation.

Thailand is to a certain extent matriarchal. Women can influence behind the scenes, however deferential they may appear to be towards the male gender in other ways. The man may look macho but it is the woman who wears the trousers. The Thai language frequently gives clues to cultural peculiarities and differences. The word for a military commander literally translates as "*mother* of force" showing that, even in the army, strength and military might is seen as a feminine characteristic. There are other examples in *Thailand Take Two*.

The woman is in charge of the home and handles the finances. In most families, the woman is responsible for the children's discipline. There are exceptions, sometimes violent, but fathers typically prefer not to get involved.

Discipline within the family can appear lax to the western eye. Children come across as being spoilt and allowed to have their own way. Thais seem to have difficulty balancing caring for a child with occasionally having to say no. They take a more laissez-faire attitude to bringing up children than other nationalities. It is, once more, the influence of *mai bpen rai* and avoiding arguments.

It was a very embarrassing moment for the English couple who had invited Dao and her six-year-old son to help them celebrate their wedding anniversary at a local restaurant. They had met Dao while on holiday. It was their first time in Thailand and they appreciated her showing them around.

Pomelo, her son, had asked for a coke with ice. Then he wanted more ice. And more and more. His glass was filled to the brim. Dao tried to explain that the coke would spill over if more ice was added. He was having none of that logic. He wanted strawberries but then refused to eat them. Dao offered them around the table but he snatched them back and kicked over two chairs in a fit of temper. Dao rang her husband and asked him to come round but he said he had agreed to go fishing with friends. She dragged him to the toilets where he could still be heard screaming and shouting. When they returned twenty minutes later, there were bite marks on Dao's right ankle. Mosquito bites, she said.

The Thais at the restaurant did not seem particularly surprised at the chairs being knocked over and the screaming. It rather spoilt Pat and Barry's lunch though. They were visibly shocked by Pomelo's behaviour.

French families are generally even stricter with their children than the English. They believe in enforcing manners at an early stage. They will shout and even slap to ensure that the message for the need for good manners is understood. Children are taught both at home and at school to be polite with strangers, to behave correctly at table, and not always insist on having their own way. They are expected to do as they are told. In twinning exchanges between France and England, for example, you will find that at the formal functions the French have separate tables for the children. The French do not involve their children in adult activities or conversation. They are meant to be seen and not heard. Thai families would not segregate the children. To them, one family means one family.

When the English return the hospitality the following year, adults and children sit at the same table. Thai families would do the same. For them, it is important that the family be kept together. Some would wonder if there are links between how children are raised and the adolescent and adult crime rates in various countries.

The apparent and stated emphasis in juvenile correction centres in Thailand is on rehabilitation rather than on punishment. Sometime it succeeds; sometimes it does not. The more street-wise kids are practiced in taking advantage of the enlightened but soft approach. Although conditions in penal institutions can be harsh, discipline is not rigorously enforced in junior detention centres. Thais dislike coming across as creating conflict. You will see smiles in Thai prisons, at times you'll hear laughter and humour from inmates and guards. Video calls on Skype are allowed. But you won't see individual televisions in the cells, there is no choice of meals, and toilet facilities are primitive. Prisons are not hotels. Conditions may appear tough but the atmosphere is not an unhappy uncaring one.

Daily announcements by the village headman over the village loudspeaker system show how concerned Thais are for those in the community. Regular information is given on school events, children's activities, and hobbies for the elderly. People are reminded that there is a free lunch for pensioners or that a new fitness class is about to start.

The headman of each village, the *puyaibaan*, is elected by the community and is responsible for the smooth running of his *tambon* (district). His official functions include the maintenance of voting and resident registers and the resolution of minor disputes. He is also an important part of the communications loop between the district government, the provincial government, and ultimately the national government. The eyes and ears of what is going on locally in the community.

China has a very similar system with its neighbourhood and village committees. The *puyaibaan* in Thailand is pro-active in local activities. The more dynamic communities are those with a dedicated and trusted village headman. Everyone knows and respects him. He knows everyone in the area.

Thailand, as a country, runs smoothly through its community structure. It has a history of coups and political unrest but an uncanny ability to run administrative systems smoothly throughout those periods. Even when a government is removed from office, it is business as usual in much of the country it seems. If you had no access to the news you would wonder if any disruption had actually taken place. People still smile and carry on enjoying themselves.

People help each other in many ways. Although a drainage canal is local authority property, homeowners will make repairs to it if it is on adjoining land and to do so would benefit the neighbours. For a more major cleaning, a task force may be organised and spend a morning working voluntarily together. A party usually follows.

In one village, a compost heap had been established with everyone bringing their garden and farm waste. A year later and the composted material was shared out. Community participation and thoughtfulness for others, *greng jai*, can be quite strong. If this idea of cooperation was developed more widely, it might alleviate the seasonal problem of smog in some parts of Thailand. In the North particularly, the practice of slash and burn, where fields are burned prior to the next crop, regularly causes breathing difficulties and hospitalisation. Composting or ploughing-in after harvest might be better.

Surplus fruit or vegetables from your garden are shared with those living near you. It is more than a gesture; it is a standard response to which Thais would never give a second thought. If a villager is not at home, the food is left in a parcel on the gatepost. This is *Nam jai* in action, caring and sharing.

Giving is reciprocal in Thailand. If a gift is given, you will receive something in return at some other time. The Thais are somewhat particular in keeping to this rule of give and take which they call *sam nuk bun kun*. Not to respond to a gift would be unthinkable. They don't want to be in your debt and want to share their *nam jai* with you. You get a feel for how often and how much.

Community interests can overrule laws and regulations. Agreements can go by the board. What is considered best for the family or community will always take precedence over any binding contract. Village elders decide how the local community runs. It is usually successful as the more snobby members find themselves held back in public meetings by a general consensus of those keen to see the village and community develop.

Even with a discussion on family and community, we see how hierarchy, face, cheating, religion, and respect are all inter-related.

Chapter 6

The End of a Life

He arrogantly insisted on some petrol money to go to the hospital.

Dta Sompet had been bitten by a neighbour's dog and needed an anti-rabies injection as a safeguard. Whether the dog was provoked or not was difficult to tell. Anyway, the owner paid for the hospital fees and the petrol. But he thought his demand for having his petrol costs paid was a little over the top. The families smiled when they saw one another but it was not the smile of close friends. It was the automatic Thai smile.

As *farangs*, we may not notice the coldness of the snub but then the Thai smile is never easy to understand. Years went by with only a few words being exchanged. However, as we shall see, events would change that. If only for a short time.

I saw Dta Sompet most days. He was either reading his newspaper or doing some light gardening. He would always stop for a chat when neighbours walked by. I usually joined in the chitchat and banter. Thais love to gossip and joke. Lately he had been unwell and had been taken to the hospital for check-ups. Occasionally, I would see him reading his newspaper in the shade of his garden. We would exchange a few words but he was not his usual self. He was not as energetic as he was before.

Whenever I asked his family if he was getting better, I was told he was okay. A standard reply from a Thai. They did not want people to be sorry for them. This attitude of caring for the feelings of others, *greng jai*, is the Thais' routine response to not putting you to any trouble. But I was genuinely concerned for his health.

I buttonholed his granddaughter, Renu, as she was riding her motorbike to university. She told me he was dying and that the surgeons could not operate on his kidney problem because of his age.

He was eighty-three years old and was being sent home to die.

I found him a kindhearted man. His youngest daughter, Fai, was divorced and lived alone above her shop a few hundred metres away. It had been burgled twice. Until he became very ill, he had slept over every single night of the year without fail to protect her. Caring for other members of the family is a strong Thai trait.

We saw him that evening. He was lying on one of the long wooden teak benches that the Thais like to have in their homes. They are expensive because they are well crafted and ornate but Westerners find them uncomfortable even when provided with lots of cushions. He was propped up to stop him falling to one side and was cheerful enough. He smiled as we entered and understood what we were saying, very light-hearted stuff. We had often shared a joke together.

But now he was not able to talk. Only his wife, Khun Fon, and eldest daughter, Khun Faa, were with him when we visited, but many close friends had popped around during the day for a short while. Perhaps bringing a soft drink or something they thought he might be able to eat. There were smiles and chattering amongst the visitors, but no assumption that he was going to survive.

The family was still concerned that they were causing an inconvenience to his visitors. Always, the family thanked them for coming round to see him. Always, the response from his friends was the same: *"Mai bpen rai krap."* (literally, it doesn't matter.) It seemed an inappropriate response to their thanks but it is the correct one in Thailand. It wasn't that they didn't mind. They cared a lot. The meaning was that they did not need to be thanked for visiting their old and beloved friend. *Mai bpen rai* can have many different shades of meaning. In the context of a man dying, it still seemed odd to a western ear.

The next day he was moved upstairs and laid on a mattress on the floor of what one might call the "shrine room." This room is typical of many Thai homes. In one corner stands a Thai altar with some Buddha images, flowers, candles, and photos of revered monks. In presenting sticks of incense to a Buddha image, you cup three sticks in your hand and *wai*. On one side of the altar, there is a small plate of food and a glass of water that are replaced each day. This is a symbolic gesture much like decorating Christian altars with flowers.

Many family photographs are hung on the walls, together with pictures of past kings. There are always photos of the present king, often from previous years' calendars. On another wall are stacked many magazines and books gathered over the years. Most of the books are cartoons, or school or university entrance texts. Apart from two small teak chairs, the room is otherwise not furnished. It is a place for quiet contemplation, not one for ordinary everyday use. Victorian front parlours in England were similar. Used only for resting a coffin or for very formal occasions.

Dta Sompet had not been laid in his own bedroom. For a Westerner it was a strange sensation to realise that his being laid on a mattress in the shrine room was signaling to everyone in the village that our friend and neighbour was dying. He would end his days in this room.

In the West, we talk of a deathbed. In hushed tones. There is little conversation and the atmosphere is sad. We may try to convince ourselves that there is a slim chance of recovery.

Thais are under no such illusion. To them, death is the final part of the normal life cycle. It may come unexpectedly but is regarded as a perfectly natural event. There is sorrow and mourning but it is neither morbid nor solemn.

Dta Sompet was able to drink liquids and Khun Faa was spoon-feeding him some weak rice soup. The wife of one of his nephews was massaging his limbs and wiping off the sweat that was building up on his body. Someone else helped hold him so that he could be given some medication. The Thais can be very caring and comforting. They will do all they can to ease any sort of suffering.

A monk arrived later in the evening and held a short prayer session. Khun Faa's husband lifted Sompet's thin frame so that a white ribbon could be wound round his wrist as a symbol of blessing and protection, the *sai sin*. The monk said some comforting words. Dta Sompet was conscious and seemed quite reassured and contented at the monk's presence. He was still too frail to speak but seemed to know what was going on and was quite at ease.

Over the next fourteen days, there was a constant stream of visitors to the home and the monks came a few times. It was very much open house where you just quietly walked in and went up the stairs to where he lay. The door was always open. If Dta Sompet was sleeping people would just chat, the usual small talk. Everyone would help in any way they could. Just tidying up or handing out glasses of water or light refreshment.

Western way would be respectful but more formal; letting the family cope on their own most of the time. But this is Thailand and Dta Sompet's friends would never let him be alone at this time. They came every day. Overnight there would always be one or two family members sleeping on the floor near him, not in their own bedrooms.

Then one morning around ten o'clock there seemed to be an almost continuous stream of friends and neighbours arriving by either foot or motor cycle, and then leaving after just a few minutes. A sign that he had died. The mattress on which he had been sleeping during his last few days had been removed. The doctor and undertaker were yet to arrive. Dta Sompet was now lying, covered completely in a white cloth, on the bare floor of the shrine room.

Condolences were offered to his wife, Khun Fon, and the family, but not in the same formal way as in the West. By just being there and showing that they cared, few words were needed. Just a slight smile of compassion. No crying. No tears.

As I left, I heard the *puyaibaan*, (village headman) announce our neighbour's death on the village loudspeaker system. It was half past ten. Dta Sompet had been dead for less than one hour. Yet around twenty people had already visited his house. In small villages in Thailand, word travels fast. Communities are closely knit. In some provinces, the family starts wailing as a way of announcing the death. That did not happen here. Customs differ depending on province and region.

Dta Sompet and Khun Fon had lived in this village for most of their lives. Both their families were well known and well liked. They were part of the community. They belonged.

The family concept is strong in this country. It is very important to a Thai to keep in close contact with the family. To always be there for one another. Families often live in the same compound or at least very close by. Thais like to live in close communities.

This bereavement showed me the strength of family and neighbourliness in Thailand. The community that joined in during the happier days was there in equal numbers during this period of sadness.

Ruam took; ruam sook, sharing the good and the bad times together.

The wife of the neighbour whose dog had bitten Dta Sompet sent round her factory workers with chainsaws to help fell some *lamyai* (longan) trees near the house. Half a dozen men made short work of clearing an area that I later realised would be used for the erection of six large awnings. The space would be needed to cater for the large number of people coming over the next week to pay their respects.

Any bitterness that had accompanied the dog-biting incident was now clearly in the past. The two families would, however, never be exceptionally close.

That evening, and for the next two nights, a monk arrived to start the funeral rites, holding the traditional fan, the *talapatr*, in front of his face while chanting from the *sutras*, the holy scriptures.

These mantras are a means of passing merit to the deceased. Prayers are about the impermanence of life. Although the presence of only one monk is acceptable, particularly immediately after death, the usual tradition is that funeral rites are observed with an even number of monks. This rule of even numbers is not always followed. Later in the week, there were usually six or eight monks in attendance.

You may observe, when you are in Thailand, that traditions, customs, and indeed regulations, are not automatically adhered to. Funerals can take place with an uneven number of monks and parts of ceremonies are omitted. You are unlikely to get a satisfactory answer if you ask for an explanation. The truth is that Thais value freedom above all else. They will adapt and alter to suit what they want to do, but they will not tell you that. This is why it is extremely difficult to give clear-cut details of traditions and events that apply throughout Thailand.

Death is regarded as the most significant part of the Thai life cycle and monks spend a significant part of their time at these ceremonies. Partly because he had died on a busy Buddhist holiday, and partly because he was so well known in the four hamlets that form this village, different monks arrived each evening.

There is no single funeral ceremony as in the West. The *gnap sop*, funeral rite, starts with the monks arriving on the day of death and continues until the cremation. Monks also attend when the cremated bones are interred or scattered on the waters of a river, and again when the 100 day memorial service, the *tambon roi wan*, is held.

Many people came to Dta Sompet's home in this first week. The front door was always open during daylight hours. The format for visitors was broadly the same. On entering the home for the first time, you light an incense stick, put it in your hand in a *wai* like gesture, and place it in front of the photo of the deceased in the entrance hall. Moving upstairs to the room where the coffin is resting, you first pay respect to the Buddha shrine. Three *wais*. Then, to the coffin, one *wai*. Unlike the normal *wai* of greeting from a standing position, these *wais* are completed by making a full *wai* from a kneeling position, then putting both hands on the floor, and lowering your head right onto your hands. You then sit on the floor facing the monks, with your feet pointing away from them. The very infirm sit on chairs at the back. There were usually around thirty family, friends, and neighbours present at any one time.

All Thai homes have a *san phra bhumi* (spirit house) in the garden in honour of ancestors. This is a small half-metre square structure on a pedestal, which looks rather like a miniature sala or garden pergola. Usually with the long over-hanging roof so typical of Thai temples.

After Dta Sompet's death, the custom of the family offering three incense sticks to the Buddha image inside the *san phra bhumi* continued. This was out of respect for those who had previously lived in the house. It was not specifically related to the present death. As we have seen, Thais dislike shows of anger and people speaking loudly. In front of or near a spirit house, it would, they believe, cause offense to the spirits, bring bad luck, and not be following proper etiquette. So, people are quiet and respectful when they are near spirit houses. No one will offend the family spirit and harmony will be maintained. This animistic belief is robustly followed in Thailand. Some Buddha icons are reputed to have magical powers of healing and creating wealth. Buyers of lottery tickets can be seen consulting such images at some of the famous shrines in Bangkok. Generally, though, they are meant to be representative and reminders of the Buddha's teaching, which is the reason you *wai* them.

Friends and neighbours came and went throughout the day. After paying their respects they would move into the garden to chat and eat. In the evening mourners did the same though around thirty or so would stay in the shrine room for the rites when the monks were present.

The men always sit in front of the ladies during the religious service. But one evening a rather hi-so lady (or so she thought) sat next to her husband, with men sitting behind her. She was a little over-dressed too, with more than an acceptable amount of jewellery for a bereavement. No-one commented, that would not be the Thai way, but the breach of protocol and manners was certainly noted. With a smile, of course. Thais try not to let you know what they are thinking. She and her husband, Damrong, only came to the house on that one occasion.

Each evening, some refreshment is given to the monks. Always by a man and always with a *wai*. The rite starts with chanting by a village elder before the monk begins his part of the ritual. The man who is chosen for this position is always well versed in how the *wat* (temple) conducts its services. Most Thai men will have spent some time in the monkhood and he would have been one of the temple's more devoted followers. Most men will stay a few weeks or a month at least. In the past, they were encouraged to stay for the whole of the four month rainy season, the "rains retreat." Some nowadays find an excuse to leave after a few days claiming pressure of work.

Monks do not *wai* lay people but novices often forget the newly learned rules. They frequently *wai* their parents and elders in their earlier days in the monkhood and refer to themselves as *pom* when it is mandatory for monks to use the word *atama*.

During most of the rite conducted by the monks, your hands are held in a permanent *wai*, though it is acceptable, if tired, to make a formal *wai* to the monks and then cup your hands in your lap.

Towards the end of the service, several bottles of water and glasses are handed to some of those present. Half the water is poured into the glass while the monks are chanting and the rest when they finish. The first half that is poured is a token gesture and is done to pray that the deceased has good karma. You are performing this duty of pouring water for his benefit after death. The second half is to pray for your own karma.

Karma is the Buddhist belief that whatever you do comes back to you. If you do good, something good will happen to you in thefuture, either in this life or the next. The reverse is also true.

Before they leave each evening, the monks are presented with baskets containing food, drink, and maybe a flower and some toiletries for their personal use. The baskets are carried by the mourners down to a car taking the monks back to the *wat*. The gifts gain merit for the family and the deceased. As monks do not have money to buy food and other essentials this is effectively a form of alms giving. Chatting, either upstairs where the coffin lies or in the garden, will continue after the monks have left; conversations can be about anything under the sun and not just about Dta Sompet's life. The atmosphere is much more informal and jovial than in the West, but there is no less respect.

Thais believe it is better for the family not to be left alone. The western view is that a stream of friends popping in unannounced every day is not giving the family private time to grieve alone and come to terms with its loss. Being with this family and sharing its grief showed clearly how different the Thai and western cultures are. It is for you to judge the merits, advantages, and disadvantages of the two styles of bereavement. We may think their customs strange; they don't always understand ours.

The casket is bedecked with flowers and twinkling coloured lights are draped around it. A tray with a small plate of food and a glass of water is placed next to the coffin and refreshed each day.

The idea of placing food next to the coffin was once questioned by a *farang* during a funeral in Bangkok.

Why do that? He's not going to be able to eat it.

He got an instant response from the Thai.

You put flowers on the grave. Is he able to smell them?

Only once did I see any tears shed in public. Dta Sompet's eldest granddaughter, Ning, arrived from Bangkok during the monks' chanting and broke down while hugging her mum and grand-mum. She worked in the city as an IT consultant but spoke to her parents and the family several times a week, coming "home" every other month. Thais habitually work a long distance from the family home as well-paying jobs are scarce outside Bangkok.

Ning composed herself quickly. Thais believe it frightens the deceased to see his family cry. They always try to hide their emotions.

As wreaths from groups and organisations arrive, they are placed behind the monks' chairs and remain there during the evening services. If members of the family are employed by companies or the government then it is usual for that organisation to send some representatives with a wreath. The fact that the deceased was not a member of that organisation himself is not relevant.

One rather moving scene was when a group of some dozen young university students arrived on motor cycles dressed in sober colours to pay respects to the family and kneel in front of the coffin. These teenagers, from Renu's university, came to offer her comfort and support.

The sense of community is so strong in Thailand that it was perfectly normal for these students to get together and contribute to the purchase of a wreath with money they could barely afford. Renu was a fresher student and had been in college for only two weeks.

I am not sure that would happen in the West.

No lotus flower was placed in Dta Sompet's hand and no coin placed in his mouth. Traditions vary throughout Thailand and they are often modified to some extent, nothing is inflexible. There are no fixed rules of funeral etiquette. Sompet's was a typically middle class Northern Thai funeral.

Particularly if the family's house is too small or has no garden, the coffin may be kept at the local *wat*. The rituals are very similar. The family would not usually stay overnight. If they did, several members of the close family would keep vigil. Sometimes monks join them for part of the evening.

Light refreshments for the mourners are provided each day until the cremation. This can be two days, three days, or a week later. It depends on the family's position and wealth. A royal funeral can last a year or more. The higher up the social ladder you are; the longer the number of days between death and the final rite at the funeral pyre.

For poorer families, the corpse is placed in an inner plywood coffin within the ornamental casket and cremation takes place within three days of death. At the crematorium, the casket is dismantled and taken away. The plywood coffin containing the body is then rolled into the fire chamber. In rural areas, the tradition is for the coffin to be placed on a funeral pyre in the open air. For families that can afford it, formalin is used to slow down decomposition and allow a more extended period of mourning.

If the intention is for the body to be donated for medical science, it is kept in a refrigerated unit behind a screen. It is only put in the casket at the end of the religious ceremonies and before being placed in the hospital ambulance. During the rites, the empty coffin is still revered and adorned with flowers and wreaths, although the actual corpse is preserved behind the screen.

For Dta Sompet, members of the community did not just offer their condolences. They helped wherever they could. Four hundred chairs were brought in and arranged under six marquees and awnings. Funerals are regarded as social events where the entire community can take part. For the first seven days, food is provided three times a day for those present. Not everyone came to every meal but cooking and distributing up to 1000 meals over a period of a week takes some organising. Music plays outside but that is turned off when the monks arrive.

There was only one person who seemed to come only for the meals. I never saw him helping and, although he was not ostracised or made to feel unwelcome, he never seemed part of the group. The Thais rarely, if ever, directly cold-shoulder you.

Nobody really leads or is in charge; everyone assumes the rôle to which he or she is best suited. When someone noticed it was getting rather hot in the tents, a couple of men got in a truck and brought back some fans from the *wat* to hang from the roof. No one told them to do so. They just did it. When the driveway was looking rather the worse for wear from the volume of traffic, a load of shingle arrived and was spread over the area. A neighbour cleared a weedy area on the verge outside the house. She was not asked. She just did it. Thais involve themselves in their communities, but as individuals. You may notice little structure in how something is organised. Individualism is a Thai characteristic that appears enigmatic when compared with their willingness to engage in local events – whether funerals, fetes, or other social gatherings.

At Dta Sompet's funeral, no formal paid caterers were employed. The community saw it as its responsibility and duty.

Men were chopping up meat; women were preparing and cooking. The men were making baskets of bamboo; the ladies were decorating them. It was very much a community event even though there was no overall direction. It appears coordinated because the traditions are well known and precisely followed. In the West, community strength evolves from working together in a structured and possibly planned way. In Thailand, it works – and works well – by being more spontaneous with individuals aware of what needs to be done. You don't hear orders being given in group activity.

The baskets were used as containers for the offerings to the monks and for general decoration around the coffin. Each day motor cycle sidecars arrived with bags of ice and bottled water. Ingredients for meals arrived on all sorts of transport from pedal bicycle to sidecar to pick-up truck. Lottery sellers came round during the day. Electioneering pamphlets were handed out. The candidates were among the mourners.

On the day before the cremation and after the monks had completed the chanting of the funeral service for that day, the coffin was brought from the house into the garden. As the coffin was moved out of the room, all the men stood. It was the only time that this was done in the presence of the deceased. The monks stood nearest the coffin and offered prayers. The men remained standing, partly to screen from the ladies present the movement of the coffin as it was being manhandled down the stairway to the garden. Everyone followed and the rite continued in the garden. The coffin was placed on a catafalque, to form an elaborate, tall, and ornate pyramid-like structure.

In some parts of Thailand, the tradition is for the coffin to be taken out of the house by a route not normally used. A wall may be broken down to make an exit or a rear door may be used. An older custom is for banana leaves to be placed on the floor so that the deceased is not being carried over the normal bare floor. This did not happen here and these practices are becoming rarer.

Although booked with the authorities, no one wanted to confirm the actual time of the cremation. To a Westerner, this can appear as Thai evasiveness. To the Thai, not being precise is due to not wanting to be forceful. "It starts at 1pm" could imply that you are expected to go whether you want to or not. Thais are just not that assertive. They speak indirectly and don't like taking responsibility for giving out information which may prove inaccurate.

When you go to a wedding in Thailand, you mingle with guests for a few hours. A house-warming, *tambonbaan,* will last a morning and perhaps there will be a small party in the evening. Funerals are not scheduled for just the one day as they are in he West. The funeral rites start at death and continue until cremation. It is no surprise then that you will meet more friends and neighbours during this time than on any other occasion. You may pop in one day and get chatting with a few friends, the next day you will meet some new neighbours over lunch. People are coming and going all the time. You get to know a lot of people who live in the local community and they get to know you. The Thais will feel happy and at ease that you are fitting in to their culture and society as well as paying your respects to the deceased and his family.

When the rites were over, close family kept vigil at the coffin during the rest of the evening. A small group of friends and neighbours stayed in the garden overnight chatting, watching a Thai soap on a screen erected in the garden, or playing cards. (Technically illegal in Thailand as the police will assume you are playing for money.) The deceased is never left alone. Inside and outside lights are not switched off at night.

The next day, from early morning, more and more people arrive until the garden is full to capacity. One neighbour built a makeshift bridge over a drainage ditch between his property and Dta Sompet's in order to connect the two gardens and allow more space for the large number of villagers attending. The man whose dog had bitten Dta Sompet opened his factory yard to provide more car parking space. He had not been asked to do so. This *greng jai* idea of not seeking favours from other people stops Thais from making such requests. Neighbours use their initiative to know what they are required to do. Thais can at times be dogmatic and stubborn, but they are not an assertive people. They won't explicitly ask for favours.

Every seat is taken. Lunch is provided for everyone by the ever-efficient helpers, all members of the local neighbourhood. As an exercise in logistics, it is carried out flawlessly. Following the traditions of centuries, it is perhaps not surprising that everything runs so smoothly.

Before the procession starts, the monks conduct a service upstairs in the shrine room but it is now also relayed to villagers gathered outside in the garden. No one minds Sompet's beloved dogs barking during the monks' chanting and indeed some friendly chatting is not taken as being disrespectful. How much money this was costing was a topical conversation piece. Listen to Thais speaking and you will notice how often numbers and prices crop up in everyday speech.

After the prayers, mourners walk in procession to the crematorium a few kilometres away. As a final show of respect, they pull the coffin through the hamlets of the village. At the head of the cortege, two of Renu's friends from university carried a framed photograph of Dta Sompet. They were followed by the local school band. They had wanted to participate. Walking two abreast, as it was a funeral, the monks come next. They take hold of the two ropes attached to the bier as that is symbolic of their taking the deceased to the final rite. The weighty structure on which the coffin is placed is actually hauled by the mourners who are walking behind the monks. The family is nearest the coffin. By tradition, the eldest son is the first person to start pulling the bier before the rest of the mourners take up the strain of hauling the cortege.

The procession is well organised. Traffic is discretely controlled and anyway all vehicles make way for the cortège. There are no traffic lights in the village; but if there were, all cars would stop and let the procession through, whether the light was on green or red. Showing outward respect is of the essence to a Thai. During the procession, two guys have to use long bamboo poles to hold up electric wires for the coffin to pass under. For some reason electricity and telephone cables in Thailand are never pulled taut. Posts always look very insecure, are never completely vertical, and the wires sag dangerously.

Only the very infirm and elderly did not walk in front of the coffin. They were waiting at the crematorium for the arrival of the cortège.

The widow was just a few years younger than Sompet and did not attend the cremation because of the superstition that it would forebode her own death. She remained at home with two or three close friends for company. Thais can be very superstitious. You will often not be able to rationalise with them or use logic. For example, a husband will invariably sleep on his wife's right side and neither will sleep with their heads facing west, whatever they may tell you.

People of the Northern provinces adopt different customs from those in Bangkok and the centre of Thailand. Dta Sompet's funeral would have cost around 300,000 baht which is the typical amount spent for a middle class *Lanna* (Northern Thai) family. Most funerals are not that elaborate. Thais will often borrow at extortionate rates to give the deceased a good send-off. Or, as they see it, to gain merit so that the deceased has the best chance of taking good karma to his next life.

Many Thais have insurance to cover funeral expenses and the full costs are defrayed by the custom of mourners giving an envelope containing cash to the deceased's next of kin. Some cynics have suggested that this can be more than the cost of the funeral but that is somewhat exaggerated. This village has, in addition to the envelope scheme, a "funeral club" where each family pays 20 baht when someone dies. Even those who could not attend the rites were thus able to contribute.

As the cortege arrives at the cremation site, those waiting near the funeral pyre stand. During the first part of the cremation service, the family selects some of the high-ranking people and officials present and gives them saffron robes so that they can offer them to the monks as alms and merit. They are placed on the table around which the monks are standing. The merit given will be transferred to Dta Sompet.

Damrong, the husband of the lady with lots of jewellery on show at one of the evening prayer sessions, was asked to present a robe. As a teacher, he was an obvious choice to be included amongst the great and the good at this ceremony. The rules of hierarchy were being followed but he did not really seem to fit in.

The monks pray for good karma and symbolically pour water down a chute towards where the coffin lays, the ceremony of *sat nam*. There is a blue tape, the *bhusa yong*, leading from the table on which the robes are placed to the coffin. This signifies that the gifts of the robes to the monks are considered as having come from the deceased.

In some provinces, you will hear the soft chant.

Sleep well, go to places you like, no need to worry about us.

The young teenagers who are present circulate among the mourners offering drinks of cold water. Everyone has a rôle to play and the tasks are conducted without fuss or any apparent issuing of directions. Because everyone is aware of the traditions, the funeral is carried out meticulously and naturally. It is much like watching a well-organised and disciplined military event.

Some mourners, those higher in the hierarchy and who had helped during the last few weeks, were given a small envelope with cash inside. A sign of gratitude from the family as it would have been impossible to thank everyone. The guys that helped erecting tents and chain-sawing trees in the full sun, the ladies working over their hot open-air stoves preparing meals, neither expected nor wanted any explicit display of thanks.

All the mourners were given a lotus blossom to place on a tray near the coffin as they filed past. This part of the ceremony was also the family's opportunity to *wai* each person present for attending and paying their last respects. Often a small gift or religious text is given to each mourner, though that does not always happen in the Lanna province.

In some regions, the flowers are thrown directly into the flames of the funeral pyre.

The final act before the actual cremation is to view the body. In the West, this is done shortly after death when the body is first placed in the coffin. After a few days, the casket is then sealed and there is no further viewing. In Thailand, you don't view the body until just before cremation. It is the last farewell.

The corpse is laid on a ceremonial table. Family and friends file past. Dta Sompet was dressed completely in white, his hands formed in the traditional Thai *wai* position. Each person pours lustral (holy) water from a ladle onto the right side of his body. Members of the family are the first to make this gesture of seeking forgiveness for any wrongdoing the deceased may have committed. It is also seen as the mourners asking Dta Sompet to forgive them for any offense they may have caused him in his lifetime.

Dta Sompet's son-in-law, in a very moving gesture, held Faa and Fai tightly as he led them away from the last time they would see their father. Friends and neighbours continued to file pass the body and complete the ceremony.

The stiff hands, still in the *wai* position, are eased down so that the coffin lid can be put in place. The coffin is taken to the pyre, together with the tray of lotus flowers, and the local Member of Parliament, as the senior person present, presses the button to start the cremation.

Everyone starts to leave once the flames begin to consume the body. Nobody looks back towards the burning fire. To do so would, according to Lanna belief, be an invitation for ghosts to follow you home. The soul is released from the body on cremation.

Fireworks are then usually set off to scare evil spirits and to announce that the funeral is over. Dta Sompet was a dog lover and fireworks scared his dogs. In deference to his wishes, only a few fireworks were let off.

Three days later, members of the family and close friends gathered the bones from the funeral pyre. They were placed in an ornamental jar to await the arrival of four monks for the final service. Although more usually the bones are put in a vault or scattered on the flowing waters of a river, the family had decided that their grandfather would have preferred a tree to be planted over his remains. They believed that he would have appreciated that choice, as it would provide shade for those who come to mourn at the cremation site in future.

When the prayers ended, Dta Sompet's bones were finally laid to rest.

Seven days after the cremation there was a *tambon* or merit ceremony at the house with eight monks attending. Most of the village came either for the early morning rite or for some time during the day. In most regions of Thailand there will be another ceremony in 100 days, the *tambon roi wan*, hundred-day merit. That is held at the *wat* and is attended by family and very close friends. Neighbours and villagers would not normally be present.

The morning service, in the shrine room, took the usual form except that each mourner put some blessed rice into the monks' alms bowls, which were linked by a white cord to a photo of the deceased. That cord was also connected, through an open window, to the truck that Dta Sompet used to drive. In the back of the truck, also attached to the cord, was the bicycle that he rode.

Looking at the bike, you could visualise Dta Sompet cycling to his daughter's home every night. So concerned had he been to ensure that she was safe following the burglary so many years ago.

After the monks had left, the family deliberately created a happier mood. There was music, some dancing, and lots of light banter. You may have noticed similar shows of respectful gaiety at Nelson Mandela's funeral in December 2013. Different peoples; different cultures.

The point was being made that Dta Sompet was no longer with us and that life must go on.

Chapter 7

How do Thais see Foreigners?

"Stupid *farang*," Samrak's words stopped all conversation in the crowded room immediately. Her western husband was noticeably trembling.

Why doesn't my husband know that when I ask for money for the veterinarian's bill for the family's sick buffalo, I am really asking for money so that my brother can buy a new and more powerful motorbike. Don't foreigners understand what Thais are really saying?

Why can't he realise that the buffalo is not sick, the bill couldn't possibly be 60,000 baht. Has he no idea of medical costs in a developing country? Vets are expensive throughout the world; but, in a country where the average daily wage is 300 baht, even a vet's bill would never be that high. Farangs always seem to think as if they are still living in the West.

I'm saving him from humiliation and loss of face. It's sweet talking, all we Thais do it. It's not lying, not as I think of it anyway. I am just telling him a little white lie to help him not feel boxed into a corner by my request. I know it's easier for him to accept giving money for a medical emergency than for a gift of an expensive motorcycle for my unemployed brother.

As my husband, he must provide for my family now. That includes my brother as well as my parents. Why can't he understand that my mum and dad looked after me without question when I was growing up. Now it is my turn, our turn, to repay that debt.

Maybe that is why they nicknamed me Somrak, which means "proper love" in Thai. As a member of the family, he must now help me support them and my brother. I say "must" but I really mean "want to." It is my duty. In Thailand anyway. That is what I was brought up to believe. Before I married I would do all I could to help my family. Now that I have a western husband, we should do even more for them. Farangs are richer than Thais are. Everyone knows that.

I want him to have the same nam jai that is instilled in every Thai, an instinctive generosity to other people that comes from the heart.

Honestly, I do try to explain my feelings to him. I must try harder. Perhaps we both need to try harder. We both need to understand that Thais and Westerners look at life differently.

Sometimes it is so hard and frustrating for me.

Oh, stupid Westerner.

Oh, stupid farang.

Thais believe that Westerners are not always on their wavelength and do not understand the national culture. Thais and *farangs* have worldviews of life that are not the same. Somrak was irritated but, in everyday life, Thais are not a judgmental people. They will gossip about you but they won't judge you. Too much *mai bpen rai* in their nature for that.

Thais smile and are outwardly friendly. Westerners can be reserved and more likely to be serious about matters they think are important. There is no *mai bpen rai* outside Thailand. It is as if *farangs* are tuned in to a different frequency when they communicate with Thais. And vice versa, of course.

Family values:

Somrak gives a good example when she compares her attitude to caring for her family with that of a Westerner. Thai families care for their elderly relatives by looking after them in their own home. They feel an obligation to their elders that we don't see that often in the West. Settling them in an impersonal institution like an old folks' home is not part of Thai thinking. Somrak would never consider that for her parents. That is why she lives near them in the same compound where she can care for them whenever necessary.

Relatives living far from home still keep in close contact with family members. Mobile phone companies do a roaring trade in Thailand. Thais come home for all major family occasions. Western families are not so close, preferring to meet up on formal occasions such as weddings, baptisms, funerals, and at Christmas. Thais see that as a bit limiting.

Westerners tend not to give to family in the way a Thai does. The western way is to consider the problem logically and carefully. Talking through the issues face to face with the family member and suggesting ways to resolve the difficulty. It is hardly ever an unquestioned response of giving money to the family as a matter of routine as the Thais do. Even J Paul Getty II only provided his son's kidnappers a reduced ransom of $2.8 million in 1973 when they sent him one of his son's ears in the post.

You do hear Westerners being called stupid. It is the Thai way of expressing frustration that the *farang* does not grasp how the Thai is thinking about a particular subject. Somrak believes it is her duty to support her family and is grateful that her mum and dad made sacrifices for her when she was growing up. Generally, we do not think that way. It is expected that the young will leave the nest, start their own family, and become independent. The average Thai does not understand this or why Western children are apparently allowed to criticise and argue with their parents. No Thai child would answer back. They may be stubborn, mischievous, and let off steam with their friends. They may walk away or find an excuse, however implausible it may appear to western ears. But they rarely answer back.

Foreigners value independence; Thais value their inter-dependence with family and community. *Farang* kids are encouraged to become self reliant and confident; Thais over-protect their offspring. It does not stop them having big egos but neither does it make them in any way independent.

Thais can't comprehend a *farang's* reluctance to be kind and considerate to family. They think in terms of *nam jai,* being kindhearted almost as a habit. The expat may feel he is being treated as a sugar daddy or an ATM machine, always being there to dish out money. Interestingly, one western dictionary defines generosity as "giving more than is strictly necessary or expected." Duty to one's parents is the Thais' justification for believing that paying for a family's needs is always necessary and expected.

As Somrak says of their relationship:

We will try harder. My husband and I will make an effort to understand each other's point of view and culture. It won't be easy but we will do it.

Throwing money around if done insincerely will not impress a Thai. Thais will see through that. They will love your liberality but it will not gain you their friendship or respect. The *farang* will need to work much harder than throwing money around to genuinely interact with a Thai.

Sticky shit and the attitude to money:

The Thai word for not willing to part with money is *kee niao* (literally sticky shit.) You may hear Thais refer to Westerners in that way when they are perceived to be acting in a tight-fisted or stingy manner. It comes as a total surprise to them when the same free-spending *farang,* seen to be over-paying and careless with money, appears miserly when it comes to helping a Thai family.

Most *farangs* do not bargain when buying goods. They pay the first price that is asked and treat the transaction with all earnestness. That seems stupid to a Thai. To them shopping is like a game that has to be played. To the eastern mind, it is enjoyable. It is a fun game to be played, *sanuk*. Asking for a small discount and engaging in a little conversation before purchasing something is the Thai way. Being too serious and bargaining unreasonably may, however, result in the seller aborting negotiations. He will then not sell to you at any price. Face is more important to him than any profit he may make on one sale. Thais dislike personality clashes.

The majority of Thais can trace their backgrounds back three or four generations to when their family were working the rice paddies or in similar poorly paid occupations. They can therefore readily appreciate how it feels to be broke and how important it is to have a respect for money.

Some Thais may be relatively well off now, but the greater part of the Thai people still live on an average of 300 baht per day. (The mode or modal average, the wage that the majority of the population gets.) Many can remember the poverty suffered by their grandparents and great grandparents. Most lived through the 1997 economic crisis. This history explains why they always now feel a need not to be financially vulnerable. They want just sufficient money to support themselves and their extended family.

The economic concept of the sufficiency economy is stronger in Thailand than in any other country in the Far East. The basis of this idea is to ensure the average family is financially secure but with no ambitious ideas of great wealth and power. Most of the very rich Thai are business people with a Chinese ancestry. They have Thai nationality, Thai ID cards, and at first glance, they look Thai. You only realise they are Thai-Chinese when you transact business with them. No *mai bhen rai* in their attitude then. To them, business is business and always comes first. They work as hard as the Thais but are more motivated and ambitious than the full-blooded Thai.

Construction workers particularly will take the odd day off unpaid if they know they have enough money in their pay packet at the end of the week for their daily needs. It is true of all countries but taking a "sickie" is standard practice in Thailand. They feel they are 'free" to do so. Westerners with a strong work ethic find this attitude difficult to grasp sometimes. That is a generalisation of course. The chairman of the National Coal Board, Lord Robens, when confronted with regular absenteeism in the English coal fields, asked a miner why he habitually only worked five days a week. The retort, in front of the press and TV cameras, floored Old King Cole, as he was quickly nicknamed.

"Because I don't earn enough to work for only four days." To Baron Robens, high productivity and compliance to a work ethic were unquestionable and required qualities; to the miner, his quality of life was of greater significance.

When I first came to Thailand I was told Thais were lazy. I was disillusioned of that when I saw how hard they can actually work in the hot sun. Their apparent "laziness" is linked more to their *mai bhen rai* attitude and sufficiency theories than any intrinsic laziness.

They think that the western approach to spending extravagantly may have its roots in *farangs* never having had to struggle for money, never being in the position of not knowing where the next meal was coming from. That is not always true. Thais will have difficulty believing you if you tell them that not all Westerners are well off. They are convinced we always have money to spend and don't need to be cautious in our spending. They see us being able to afford to fly thousands of miles to stay in the most expensive hotels while on holiday. That the tourist may have saved for a long time to enjoy such a holiday is not usually appreciated. Retired expats have built up savings over a lifetime and are at the mercy of exchange rate variations, usually a declining trend against a strengthening baht.

Perhaps Thais sometimes forget that their richer compatriots can afford to pay for their children to have expensive overseas education and can spend money on western healthcare services for the family. Thais own significant property portfolios abroad while foreigners here cannot own land in their own name. For ordinary Thais property laws are strict. Indeed, it was only in 1976 that a Thai husband needed his wife's permission to sell land even when held jointly in her name.

Because of language difficulties, the *farang* is not always aware that he is being overcharged. He often has no idea of what a Thai would pay for the same goods or service. Remembering what the low average wage in Thailand is should give clues to what products really cost. Prices usually follow wage rates. High wages, high prices; low wages, low prices.

I have spoken to many Thais who find it hard to believe that, as they say in their own words, Westerners can be so naive in money matters. It reinforces their view that we have more money than sense.

Eastern social attitudes:

Our different social attitudes surprise them. They dislike what they consider arrogance and being boisterous in conversation. Thais will never warm to you if you talk loudly or are too serious. *Kit mark mark*, you talk too much, is how they describe many *farang*s. It is a turn-off for them in their attempts to form friendships with Westerners. Compromising and smiling will win them over as much as understanding their customs.

We saw earlier the grave difficulties that farangs can get into by not being aware of "face" or not interpreting it in the Thai way. Thais and Westerners view the concept differently. Telling a white lie, as Somrak did when referring to the buffalo, saves everyone's face and embarrassment. Thais do not speak as directly as *farang*s. That is because they want to avoid any possible disagreement. Thais spot the white lies and understand what they are being told. We tend not to.

They do not like making formal commitments, preferring to follow their hearts and instincts. A less than frank or honest reply to a question camouflages their displeasure. Small lies, which are of little consequence, can be a means of smoothing over awkward social relationships. Thais do not like being caught out or wrong-footed. To the Thai, lying is more of a face-saving technique than a downright untruth. Western cultures tend to focus on face as a more devious attribute.

If you try to make an appointment with a Thai who does not want to see you, he will more usually say he is too busy or is out of town. You will not get a straight negative reply. He may say he will come on Friday. You and he both know he really will not turn up at all. Friday will never come. He may be tired or about to go home. He may be getting bored with his job and you have caught him at a bad moment. A Thai understands people can be fickle and simply decide they do not want to do something. You need to accept that side of the Thai character, go somewhere else, or try another day.

This is yet another example where Thais, when saving face and avoiding conflict, have a different social mind-set to the Westerner. I was once asked why Westerners don't lie to save face if it would avoid unpleasantness. I could only say that it is not in our make-up. We speak our mind more than the Thai, often careless of the consequences. Westerners lie to get off the hook; Thais to save face. It's pretty much an automatic response in their culture. We are used to direct confrontation, being frank, and speaking our minds because we regard ourselves as being equal with others. Thais do not have those concepts.

You will note many enigmas during your stay in Thailand. Their being both caring yet obstinate is one of them. They can be subservient to their parents and superiors while also showing an individual and inflexible pigheaded streak. Most of your observations when you visit will focus on the difference between how we both view our respective societies.

Thinking as Westerners, we sometimes take what someone says as gospel. Thais don't understand why we are so trusting. This is why Somrak called her husband stupid. A Thai would be more circumspect, cautious, and less trusting, though he would still be smiling as he listens to their stories. He would not assume he is being told the truth. Not all *farangs* are naïve in that way but many are.

A Hierarchy of Needs:

Thailand's theory of being as self sufficient as possible, the sufficiency economy, has links to Maslow's Hierarchy of Needs and how they see money and security in life to be the first needs to be satisfied. And most Thais are content to have just enough to live their daily lives without too much concern. A market stallholder may shut down his stall early if he has made sufficient money for that day.

Abraham Maslow's Hierarchy of Needs stresses that a basic and primary need is for sufficient food to survive. Food on the table. Next comes feeling safe and being employed and in good health. Only once these needs are met, do we move on to the desire for self-esteem, respect, and community belonging.

No wonder then that Thais are so conscious of having an adequate amount of money to live and survive. Choosing a partner, whether Thai or *farang*, is dependent on how that person can provide for his wife and family. Both the girl and her parents will consider very carefully how a prospective boyfriend will be able to look after the new family if they marry. A *farang* can often provide that need.

How do Thais See Foreigners shows that we do not view life in the same way as the Thai. In their culture, their needs in society are different from ours. Not only do they set great store by needing to feel secure but also Thais have a strong desire to feel part of their community and country, and to enjoy a laid-back lifestyle (*mai bpen rai*.)

They need to feel they are being considerate to the feelings of others (*greng jai*). An interesting example occurred recently in Bangkok. Despite numerous signs in the taxi forbidding passengers from smoking, a tourist lit up a large cigar. The driver made no comment. He had too much *greng jai* to intervene and embarrass his customer.

Some Thai women will travel abroad in search of a marriage partner. In *A Thailand Diary,* we met Louis and his Thai wife Gop. They both reached an understanding. She would care for him as he got older; he would look after her and her family financially. Their relationship works. Those that fail tend to be marriages where the husband thinks he was selected for his looks and his charms, and not the contents of his bank account. The sadness is that so many men realise their mistake too late. Better cultural awareness that Thais seek money and security more than love would have made them more vigilant. That is not to say that love is not involved.

The Thai lack of open and direct speaking and their ability to conceal their emotions and thoughts results in many Westerners not being aware of the realities of life in Thailand. The consular warnings and advice from western countries are too often so diplomatically phrased that key facts about the nation do not prominently come across.

The justice system as it applies to foreigners, the levels of corruption and cheating, the xenophobic attitude of most Thais, are not highlighted or explained. I am not suggesting western sources should be sensationalist in reporting information but they could provide better balance and put important issues in perspective. They have a duty to report fairly and enlighten visitors, tourists, and residents.

Thai internet forums are a mixed bag. Some posters paint only the idyllic side of Thailand, ignoring the downsides. Others take every opportunity to disparage and belittle the Thai or anything related to Thailand. When surfing the net check out as many sites as possible so that you do not get a one-sided view of the country and its people.

Maslow's theories are also relevant to Westerners themselves. Many expat frustrations are a sign of their not always being treated the same way as a Thai: dual pricing, land ownership, the justice system. Language problems and not integrating can be anxieties, too. This all creates for them a certain feeling of insecurity and not being in control. In Maslovian terms, the secondary needs of feeling safe and of belonging are not being met. Different cultures; different needs.

Being part of a community is another Maslovian need. Being with other *farangs* is often not sufficient compensation for not being spontaneously involved in an integrated way in the Thai community. It is, however, a common solution adopted by many *farangs*. Those that live day to day with little or no contact with Thai people could be heading for difficulties. Such a ghetto like existence is not really a long-term solution and cannot be very fulfilling. It is a contentious issue amongst *farangs*, and everyone makes his own choice on how he lives. Having chosen to live in a country, however, it is surely logical to make some efforts to understand the different culture and step towards some integration. The Thais think we should. What is really needed is mutual understanding from both the Thai and the *farang*.

Thais and friendship:

Because of their instinctive shyness and caution, Thais won't readily open up and start a real friendship and they try not to openly pry into your lives. They are not being stand-offish. It is just their natural manner and character. They'll get to know about you more through indirect and subtle questions or by asking others. If the *farang* makes the first move, he will find he is more likely to be accepted and his quality of life in Thailand will be the better for it. Provided, of course, that he does not go to extremes with too animated or boisterous an approach. Such loud behaviour will frighten off a Thai forever.

The Thais have an expression *poo dee angkrit* which refers to a *farang* who is exceptionally polite, reserved, and friendly, though perhaps a little snobbish. Like the Thai, a little aloof and reticent. The word *poo* is a term of respect in Thai, so take it as a compliment. The word *angkrit* means English but in this context can refer to any nationality. It is just that Thais perceive English people to be well mannered and shy.

Thais smile but they do not get too close too quickly. We are more formal and serious and smile only to express happiness. Thais smile because they see no reason not to. *Farangs* don't make a habit of smiling. They smile only when there is a reason.

But, when in Rome.....

Those you meet will appreciate your smiling the Thai way and will recognise you are meeting them half way in understanding their culture.

Trust:

Farangs tend to trust until they are given a reason to think otherwise. Thais do not look at it in the same way. They are even on their guard with their fellow Thais until they are confident of their honesty. Interestingly, they are more trusting of the Westerner. They will, for instance, always prefer renting a house to an expat than to a Thai because they are more certain of being paid.

Two entirely opposite world-views.

The motto, "my word is my bond" has long since disappeared in the City of London. Trust has disappeared, particularly in the banking and financial sectors. Thailand never had this idea of trusting one another in the first place. There are store detectives and cctv cameras in UK and US stores as well as in Thailand but here you will often have to pass a further security check where your goods are checked against the receipt before you are allowed out of the store. There is sometimes a further verification as you are leaving the supermarket car park. Identity cards, passports, signatures: all are checked rigorously for many transactions in Thailand and photocopies taken of the documents. Your passport will rapidly get dog-eared.

You hear "buyer beware" a lot more here than in the West. Consumer protection is not strong in Thailand. Guarantees are usually short term, often just one week. Enforcing them is never very easy. The rule is to be vigilant and not to rush into agreements or purchases.

Thais tend to be very guarded and suspicious of both their fellow countrymen and *farangs*. Listening to you and getting clues from watching your body language is how they carefully determine whether to believe you or not. It is significant that there is no trust law on the Thai statute books. Trust is a feature they are not relaxed about. For example, they realise that most written guarantees are quite worthless when it comes to trying to enforce them.

The granting and taking of credit is not widely encouraged, and this is one factor holding back this developing country. Cash transactions are common and cheques are not widely used. A banker's draft drawn on a Bangkok bank will be scrutinised cautiously by a bank manager of the same bank up-country. A manager not even trusting a draft from his own bank. As Adoon, a banker in Chiangmai, said to me:

It is only a bit of paper.

A Westerner would see that as being quite naïve and stupid. Somrak thought the same about her husband. He was being stupid for not understanding her little white lie. Adoon was being stupid for not understanding how bankers' drafts are actually cleared in the banking system.

Different cultures; different ways of thinking.

The more responsive we are to cultural sensitivities the easier we will assimilate into the Thai way of life and the more relaxed we will be visiting the country or living amongst the Thais.

Having said that, I recently read a book on expats in Cambodia. The author's conclusion is that the majority of western immigrants do not assimilate into a foreign culture. That can be true of many expats in Thailand. I believe that is a pity. Whether on holiday or in any country for the longer term, your enjoyment and feeling at ease with life in your new environment will be enhanced and less irksome if you go some way to understanding local attitudes and lifestyles.

Strangely, in reviews of the Cambodian book, there were many comments from expats belittling the whole concept of the need to integrate. Some posters on the Thai internet forums give out the same message. They are a minority but like all minorities they can give the totally wrong impression that they speak for the wider population. Unfortunately, Thais notice comments on these forums and they too can be tempted to respond by painting all *farangs* with the same brush. It must make many consider whether integrating with expats is worthwhile.

It always amazed me that, on day trips to France from the UK, there were so many tourists on the ferries that, on arrival, spent their entire day in the bars, the English fast food cafes, or shopping for cheap booze.

My view was always the same. If that is what they wanted to do, so be it. Even though the channel ports of Calais and Boulogne are close to England, there are many aspects of those two places that are very typically French if you seek them out. It is sad that opportunities to savour a French atmosphere and meet with the locals were missed.

They enjoyed their day. It is not for others to judge.

Thais do not understand our assertiveness and open frankness. They prefer a quieter, informal, friendlier approach. Their rules of status in society clash with our more egalitarian views. They consider our assertiveness as rude aggression. We may constructively criticise; they would never criticise at all. We argue; they walk away.

The average Thai has an essential sense of having to obey, to be polite, patient, and diffident. Respect and allegiance are important traits to cultivate. Enjoying life – *sanuk* – is mandatory. Work to live, not live to work.

Thais and Westerners could try to understand each other's way of life.

I will let Somrak have the last word.

Farangs don't understand our culture.

Chapter 8

Sun, Sand, Sea, and Sex

It is not true that I had nothing on. I had the radio on
(Marilyn Monroe)

Walking along Phuket's Soi Bangla or exploring the side streets of Bangkok's Patpong district, you will see a lot of human flesh on display. Girls and lady-boys showing yards of thigh sit outside the bars and nightclubs. You may be invited to go inside. The pleasures will not include listening to the radio.

Let us put Marilyn Monroe's famous wisecrack, although decades old, into a Thai context.

The country has had the label of *sun, sand, sea, and sex* for a long time and the slogan draws travellers from all over the globe every single year. Thailand benefits so much economically from being seen as a world centre of sex tourism that it is unlikely this perception will change anytime soon.

Thais accept most of what goes on in the sex industry and enjoy the knock on benefits that sex tourism brings. Many palms are greased along the way to ensure there is no interference in the practice of the world's oldest profession. Hotels, restaurants, and other leisure and entertainment businesses benefit from the foreign currency brought in by visitors eager to see for themselves all that Thailand has to offer.

While no one knows exactly how many prostitutes are working in the country, independent research suggests there are around two million. Figures showing how many clients are Thai and how many clients are tourists are not so widely available, but it is estimated that the Thai number is greater than people imagine. It is acceptable in Thai society to use prostitutes.

Although the number of girls employed in the sex industry is a small proportion of the total population, the business is operated so openly that it appears to be much higher. As in the rest of the world, the behaviour of a minority can tarnish the reputations of the majority. It is also not true that all sex workers are Thai. Many come from abroad, – some for a few weeks, some for much longer.

Prostitution was made illegal around 1960 but the laws were later changed to exclude the specific offence of prostitution. Soliciting is still against the law but applies only if it occurs "openly and shamelessly or causes a nuisance to the public." Laws in Thailand are, however, open to wide interpretation.

Provision of escort or massage services is not illegal. Pole dancing is considered a cultural art form by the authorities. Recruiting bargirls to drink with clients in a bar is not against the law. Scantily clad girls sitting in a row outside a karaoke club and smiling at potential punters are committing no offence. Calling out "Hey, you handsome man" is not soliciting but a mere expression of a man's physical attraction. Young women wearing numbered tags and sitting in a "goldfish bowl" waiting to be chosen by men sitting in rows gazing at their sexy bodies is nothing to do with paid prostitution.

The girls sit behind the glass screen watching TV and gossiping amongst themselves. There can be a lot of bitchiness and jealousy with the girls and mood swings can result in aggression. Their obvious boredom is only relieved when their number is called and they rush to get towel and soap.

Away from the "goldfish bowl" venues and the flashier nightclubs in the big cities, you find many smaller bars in every Thai town where the girls will congregate.

Although written as a novel, Stephen Leather's book *Private Dancer* gives an accurate account of the bar scene in Thailand. It describes, through the words of its main fictional characters, the devious tricks and clever tactics used by bargirls to extract money out of their unsuspecting foreign clients. It paints a colourful picture of *farangs* being routinely duped by some of the girls. Even the guys' friends can see the warning signs.

Ah, but she is not like all the other bargirls, is the reply they normally got.

Private Dancer is well worth a read as an antidote to the more glowing descriptions of Thailand which never mention the negative aspects one can experience.

There are some horror stories regarding customers being tricked by bargirls and by those more interested in "draining the ATM" of their handsome man than anything else. Thai internet forums are replete with of such anecdotes. Some may be exaggerated. Some are not. Men who were conned into a long-term liaison have been scammed out of their life savings by being too trusting of some of the girls and their associates.

Girls in the bars will order drinks and arrange to have them put on your bar tab, often to cover their own unpaid bar debts. You may not notice the prices of the drinks that you order are getting higher the longer you stay in the bar. Complaining about this will not usually get you very far. The *mamasans* (brothel madams who control, teach and look after the girls) and the bar owners, all know that most tourists will pay up regardless. If they do not, there are always a few tough guys around to persuade them. Some may be in official uniform.

Anger can erupt suddenly in the bar, with serious consequences if the girl considers she has been offended or is the victim of some slight. Thais never forget perceived insults. However long it takes, they will get even with you if they have been deceived or have lost face.

The girls get generous commissions on any drinks that are bought for them, even if they are in reality coloured water. They receive a small salary and get a proportion of any "bar fine" that the customer pays to the bar owner whenever a girl leaves with him. After leaving the bar, any money the girl receives is hers to negotiate and keep.

A trained bargirl will be an expert at making the right eye contact and playing her client to her advantage. She sees it as a long-term money transaction and to her it is just business. Her mates will be primed to cover any inconsistencies in the stories she gives to her newfound foreign friend. The *farang* may think he is the only lover, she only thinks of him as another customer that will keep coming back.

She may get her boyfriend or husband to claim he is her brother or friend. Provided cash flow is not in danger of drying up, he will play along with any sob stories she may tell as part of her scheming strategy to get as much money from her client as she can.

What the Thais find difficult to identify with is how a man's judgment seems to leave him as soon as he walks down the steps of the plane to the baggage hall. They do not understand why the *farang* does not realise that the relationship that has developed is purely a business transaction. They do not understand why they do not recognise when they are being lied to. The reality is that Thais observe body language better than Westerners. They continually interpret, as do all nationalities to some extent, their social environment and how they need to react to other people and comply with that person's culture.

Knowing a few words of Thai may help if you listen carefully to the girls' conversations. A few key words may confirm that you are being talked about in a disrespectful manner. That the relationship is not what you first thought.

Your being referred to as "*mun*," which means "it" in Thai and should only be used when speaking of things or to animals, is an indication that all is not as it should be. Most Thais would instinctively *wai* an older person. A girl not doing so when meeting you or trying to engage in conversation should tell you much about her. Such warning signs should not be ignored.

A Thai man listens to how he is addressed and would double check what he is being told. He gets to know the lady, meets her friends and family. It is not common to date a prostitute in Europe or America, why do it here? Do not believe the girls will always change.

Despite prostitution not being considered a disgrace, most Thai men would not marry a prostitute. Unlike a *farang*, they would certainly never be seen with one in public. Thais are quite forgiving but still have old-fashioned moral beliefs when it comes to dating a woman.

Not all the women who frequent the bars do so for short-time business. Some deliberately set out to catch a sole punter and turn him into a source of unending cash. They will "bait and switch." Gain his confidence first, buy him expensive gifts, and treat him as if he is in a serious relationship and not just a client. Once he believes the association is genuine, more and more financial demands will be subtly requested from him. Unless the man becomes conscious of the switch early on, he will not realise that he has been financially mugged. By which time, it may be too late and he will have to put the experience down to being too trusting.

There are foreigners living here who are now almost penniless. Technically, they can be deported at their own expense if they have little money to survive. However, the Thai authorities won't pay for deportation out of their own funds. In practice, these "alien" *farangs* go underground, under the radar.

While financial scams are perpetrated throughout the world every day, Thailand's friendly charm can sometimes lead the *farang* to a misplaced confidence and trust, and a belief that Thailand is different. There are women who set out to obtain land and houses for themselves and family using foreign money. Land cannot be owned by non-Thai nationals, so the deeds are never in their name. Some legal protection for security of tenure is available in the form of leases of different kinds but these are not that watertight. Though the girls, and sometimes also their lawyers and backers, will never disclose the pitfalls.

There is circumstantial evidence suggesting that the women conspire with élite or influential Thais in order to carry out such transactions. Though perfectly legal, these business dealings are not morally acceptable. The properties may later be sold and the girls will share the profits with those that have financed their activities.

Bargirls may have a number of fictitious names on social media and dating sites, and multiple facebook accounts. They may be playing several men at a time, while claiming that each man is the only one in their lives. It is not unusual for the woman to have several *farang* lovers in different countries and have to plan very carefully the timings of their visits to Thailand so that they do not meet one another and realise they are only one of her many clients.

The girl may be getting regular international money transfers from several sources. That is not uncommon. Money has to come from somewhere. The state does not help you if you have no work and cannot pay the bills.

Thai men would not listen to the girl's stories that she is a single woman, saving up to get herself through college, or needing money for her brother's funeral. They know it is the Thai way to make up stories that sound feasible but are untrue. A practice that avoids any confrontation and loss of face, but a fairy tale nevertheless.

What is the Thai view on prostitution? They are an easy-going people and not judgmental. Does prostitution matter to them? Is it hurting anyone? Is it their business? The Thai answer is usually no, and the *mai bpen rai* view of life kicks in. Blind eyes are turned and a practice that has been going on for centuries continues to be accepted.

While the Buddhist concept of being tolerant of others and avoiding conflict influences how Thais look at prostitution, many believers hold the view that suffering for your past deeds is an inevitable part of karma, the cycle of cause and effect called *samsara*. Are bargirls and their families now reaping the fruits of a previous bad karma and suffering the consequences? Some Thais would accept that reasoning. Others take the liberal *mai bpen rai* view, not my concern.

Though prostitution is a worldwide business, Thais have a somewhat unique perspective. There are financial and social factors that explain why it is openly condoned. Put frankly, the sex trade provides money for the family and is good for the economy. Many people who are not directly associated with the industry – whether in uniform or not – make money from the business.

There is a wide gap between the haves and the have-nots in Thailand and economic necessity can drive girls to the red light districts. The state provides little help if a family is down on its luck. Thais can only look to relatives and the local community for support. Western style welfare systems don't exist here. So to say that families sell their daughters into prostitution is to miss the point.

The trade flourishes because many of the girls are willing to work in the bars and clubs in order to provide for the family, and because society seems to condone it.

Being poor yet honest is recognised as the natural order of things in the Thai hierarchy. There is no disgrace in a prostitute sending money home to her family. As there are few opportunities for career advancement in some regions of Thailand, the girls find jobs wherever they can.

Farmers in the Isaan region of northern Thailand are amongst the poorest in the country and struggle to survive in drought-ridden conditions for most of the year. The class conscious Thai, when talking of prostitution, always associates the Isaan region with Thai prostitution. That is not entirely fair. A not insignificant number of the girls working in the trade are not even Thai.

The Thai outlook on life is rather laid-back and they help one another a lot. It is culturally accepted that girls will find money to support their families. That it may come from prostitution is never queried. If the girl is from up-country and working the bars of Bangkok, then to save face, her family would probably say she is a receptionist or a waitress. Her ability to buy a house or truck for the family would not be openly questioned, even though everyone in the village would be aware of the reality.

The girls were supported by their parents while they were growing up, going to school and perhaps university. Thai society is so family oriented that parents willingly struggle to keep their daughters in college if they have gained a place. It is no wonder that the girls feel a responsibility to repay the debt by looking after their parents when they themselves are in need. It is a filial duty deeply rooted in Thai society.

The following short video is fairly true to reality though it skips quickly over some of the downsides of expat life in Thailand. You will see and hear foreigners making fools of themselves oblivious to the reaction of the Thais they are with. It does bring out how the girls have a need for security for themselves and their families. As one woman puts it "don't want man for love, man take care of me forever." Another explains that bar girls are not bad and work because their families are poor. They feel sad inside, she says, at what they do, but try not to show it. You hear a lady describe the four men she is simultaneously chatting with over the internet. It gives, she believes, a wide choice of possible men to take care of her. One expat confides that his girlfriend's "bar level" English is a barrier in their relationship.

https://www.youtube.com/watch?v=6k6R43x6gfg

(Ctrl and click will normally work or you can type into your browser window.)

For the ordinary Thai, not involved in the skin trade, relationships between men and women are the same throughout Thailand. It is more about a woman caring for a partner and having some financial security for herself and family in return than about any expression of everlasting love. That applies to a Thai whether she is with a Thai or a *farang* partner. It has always been a feature of Thai society. Love can develop of course, but the initial concern is one of security and support from the husband.

Thai men are more likely to have sex for the first time with a prostitute rather than with a classmate or girlfriend. The position with western adolescents is the reverse. (Any pun on the word "position" is unintended.)

The polygamous practice of having more than one wife was abolished only in 1935. Before that time, a man could have any number of wives he liked: a *mia luang* (main wife), several *mia nois* (minor wives), as well as a "slave" wife, (*mia glang tasee*) purchased from her former owners.

Today, *mia nois* are an acknowledged part of society. Having a *mia noi* is partly a status symbol showing your powerful position in society. There are even rented wives, the *mia chao*. This is the custom of hiring a mistress for a period of a month or so and it first took root in Thailand in the days of rest and recuperation (R. and R.) during the war in Vietnam. Keeping a mistress for a specified time or for a longer relationship is not out of the ordinary.

Provided discretion is observed, Thai wives tolerate their husbands' keeping a second wife or having casual sex with a prostitute. Nothing is ever discussed in front of the wife and the couple still keeps up an active life together within their social circle. Their friends will be tactful. It is the Thai way. The man in effect socialises within two separate groups of friends. In this case, hoping – using a word from Kipling – that the *twain* will never meet. Friends will know of the philandering but not openly talk about it.

The wife won't like the arrangement and she obviously doesn't want to accept it. She will certainly not admit to anyone that her husband has a *mia noi*. But, of course, no one will mention it anyway. Because it is still part of Thai culture, she goes along with it. Only when having a bit on the side is viewed as improper will that change. That day has not yet come. Because Thais don't talk about this side of their culture, many expats, even those who have been here a long time, are unaware of their tacit acceptance of the *mia noi* concept.

In *Escape to Thailand* you hear Derek saying that wives no longer accept mia nois and will not tolerate a ménage a trois. He is taking everything his wife tells him at face value. She knows Thai women accept this cultural trait but Toy won't tell him that. Derek needs to get to know that Thai and *farang* women think differently.

By convention, minor wives are supported and maintained even though there is no legal obligation to do so. They have no status in law. As there can be no "divorce" from a non-registered marriage, it follows there can be no alimony. In fact, orders for child support in divorce or separation settlements are in practice not common whether marriages are registered or not. The wife and her family traditionally take care of the children following divorce or the more usual case of separation. It is not easy to divorce in Thailand; the courts will concentrate in trying to persuade a couple to reconcile. When women re-marry, it is usually with men that have been married before.

All children of the union are, however, regarded as legitimate. A main or legal wife will only sue for divorce as a last resort, usually when the liaison becomes too public. The reason normally cited is that the husband has been supporting the *mia noi* financially. The actual infidelity, as sanctioned by custom, does not seem particularly significant. Adultery by the male is not grounds for divorce, though female adultery is.

Provided that they remain financially secure, Thai wives would prefer their men to frolic with prostitutes rather than mistresses.

Taboos and superstitions abound in Thailand. Women no longer wait for a husband to start eating before she joins him. Only a few decades ago that would have been unheard of. Even today you will see women in their thirties prostrating themselves and kissing the feet of their grandparents. Thirty years ago, merely "touching" a girl could result in a fine imposed by the village headman. Unmarried couples would not be allowed alone together.

It is still familiar practice for a girl to invite her female friends along on a first dinner date! Most Thai ladies would want to date in a public place, and using a chaperone (*duenna*) is not an uncommon practice. Thai men do not find it unusual to be accompanied by a third person when out with a woman. Many Thai women would not be happy being seen with a *farang* man in a two-seat *tuk tuk* in case she could be mistaken for a prostitute. Derek's wife, Toy, categorically refused to ride in one when she first met Derek and has refused ever since.

During your stay in Thailand, you will doubtless watch the *ramvong*, the Thai national dance. You will notice that the dancers fastidiously avoid touching one another. Back in the 1930s, girls truly believed spells could be cast on them if they were not seen to be behaving in a very prim and proper way.

The registering of marriages only became popular in the 1980s in this country. Thai couples tend to marry a partner nearer their own age. Possibly, the way in which society allows men to have minor wives and visit prostitutes takes away their need to marry a much younger woman. They can have their young trophy wives and the more mature ladies at the same time, no need to re-marry a younger bride. Divorce is more common than it used to be. Having a mistress though is not the reason for most divorces or separations. Violent behaviour and abandonment of the woman and child are the usual grounds that are cited.

Business meetings may well end with a brothel visit. Government officials sent to meetings up-country will routinely be fixed up with a local beauty by the local dignitaries. That is not unique to Thailand but it is more widespread and normalised here which makes it difficult for a Westerner to refuse and not appear prudish or insensitive to local culture. The expat *farang* may feel uneasy about joining in with his fellow Thai colleagues with the regularity and openness that occurs sometimes in Thai companies. He may want to find excuses for not going along with what his colleagues take to be standard practice. He may just admit that, in his country, it is not appropriate and it would make him feel uncomfortable to accompany them. Making a joke of it and commenting with a smile would be the better means to avoid any embarrassment.

Thai women are often told what to do by their men and can appear at first glance to be quite submissive. In the family home, though, it is the woman who calls the shots. The male macho image shown to the outside world does not hold sway inside the Thai household. Factor in the woman's ability to subtly persuade and sweet talk, and a different image emerges. Look carefully at who is really exercising authority and calling the tune. Listening and observing teaches us much about Thai life.

In public, men and women are not regarded as equals in Thailand. We saw in *The End of a Life* how women sit behind the men at a funeral. Job opportunities are not as forthcoming for a woman as for a man. The women are expected to put family before career. They can fetch and carry for their men, bring them cool water, and keep the beer glasses topped up. Their duty and loyalty, nonetheless, is to their blood family and not to their husbands.

Westerners have more modern ideas of equality of the sexes.

Women cannot become fully ordained as monks in Thailand. They can be called *Bhikkhunis*, the female equivalent of a monk, but cannot enter the Sangha, the Buddhist monkhood. They can shave their heads, wear white, and become *mae jis*, but that is a lay position with no real authority.

Caring and support is what the woman needs and expects. Knowing she has some security for the future is more important than professions of love. A warning signal should sound if the handsome *farang* is told how much he is loved. Thais think he is being naïve to fall for such lines.

Thais have a reputation for sweet-talking and being persuasive. They use indirect conversation to get their own way and make people feel relaxed. Instead of asking for money directly, they will invent a feasible story and hint at your helping out. They let the foreigner think it is his idea. Bargirls are masters in this and would make Oscar winning actresses. Unlike the Thai, Westerners take a lot on trust and don't question. Thais are convinced that *farangs* are gullible and too ready to believe everything they are told. Sadly, the Thai is often right.

So how does a *farang* tell if a girl he meets outside the bar areas is genuine or not? Is she out to fleece him or is she seeking a genuine relationship?

Why not do what the Thais do? A Thai man would ask questions about a young lady's job, salary, previous jobs, education, and family. That is how Thais choose partners. Expats could use the same approach.

The question that will often floor a bargirl is, "Where did you learn your English?" Bargirls have a different vocabulary and way of speaking from Thais who have learned the language in school or university. The bargirls use slang words and the English they have learned comes from their customers and the *mamasans*. Listening carefully can tell you a lot about the girls' background and true motives.

Is her English vocabulary limited only to the essential words she needs to ply her trade? Can she hold a conversation on a topic outside the bar scene? It's a good way to establish whether the ladies you meet are in the bar for a social drink or for business.

How do hotel and restaurant staff talk to her? Do they look at her in a rather knowing way? Watch how other Thais interact with her. You may notice that when a Thai speaks he also looks out for changes in body language, those tell-tale signs that can tell whether the girl is genuine or not. A Thai's eyes can tell as much from what he sees, as his ears can tell him from what he hears.

Polite Thais will keep a respectful distance from you, will bend slightly as they pass you while you are seated, not stare at you, and they may cup their hands below their waist when talking to you as a sign of knowing your position vis a vis their own. To a *farang*, this may smack of subservience; to a Thai it is correct form and shows fine breeding and upbringing.

A sophisticated Thai lady treats being chatted up as an art form, a game that has to be played.

Let's take a more scenic path to your home. I've bought some fresh fruit for our journey.

Those who like mandarin oranges admire their ripeness, soft texture, and sweet skin. But one should be careful not to cut too deeply through the skin for the inside may be sour.

This quote from research by the anthropologist Klausner shows how well-heeled Thais play a very refined form of courtship through the wit and attitude of fun inherent in the Thai woman. *The tongue of woman is their sword and they take care not to let it rust.* (Chinese proverb)

Dressing down, as is sometimes customary in western offices, has never caught on in Thailand. In this country, the clothes you wear determine how others see you in the hierarchy. Bank tellers, teachers, and office workers dress smartly to reflect their position in society. The clothes your boss wears will indicate immediately his or her status. There is an anecdotal account of the former Prime Minister of the UK, Margaret Thatcher, asking the royal household what clothes Her Majesty would be wearing to a particular function that they would both be attending. She wanted to avoid their outfits clashing or her being accused of upstaging the monarch. According to her biographer, Thatcher was told that the Queen is not concerned what others wear in her presence.

A put-you-down which illustrates two points relevant to how Thais see foreigners. First, that you should not even think about wearing expensive clothes or jewelry in the presence of those higher than you in the hierarchy. Thais are careful to avoid this. (Though we saw an exception in *End of a Life* when Damrong's wife broke that rule.) Second, you accept what the higher classes say and do without question. You know your place.

The bargirl dresses skimpily in order to attract customers. She shows her status by the provocative and sexy "uniform" that she wears. Every Thai will notice this. Watch their expressions. Westerners don't seem to appreciate that the extreme clothes she is wearing are not like those of normal young fashionable Thais. What may be acceptable in western bars and on the beach is not all right in Thailand.

The country has a large proportion of *farangs* in their 60s and 70s in relationships with Thai women in their 20s, and only some are successful. Not all start from meeting in the bars and massage parlours of course. But many do.

The odds of a *farang* making a successful life together with a former bargirl or prostitute are very low indeed. The advice given in Thai internet forums is not usually sound, but their frequently quoted maxim, *you can take the girl out of the bar but not the bar out of the girl*, is disappointingly often true.

Sometimes a bargirl will be looking for a more secure and permanent relationship, an escape from the life she follows. Sometimes she will be interested in the association only as a financial transaction. Never easy to tell.

Do you love him, Lek.

Of course I do. He is generous with his money and looks after my family.

Yes, but do you actually love him, Lek.

You talk too much.

Lek is showing her true colours. *Poot mark mark* (you talk too much) is a favourite Thai expression meaning that her friend should not be asking that question. Her friend should have realised that there was no love involved.

Many girls have ambitions to live a western life style. They may think they have met their dream man and intend moving on from the bars. Security and having adequate money for herself and her family will be uppermost in her mind, particularly if she has been married before to a Thai and has children and family to look after. Finding a Thai boyfriend to take on such commitments may not be easy.

Parents will encourage marriages to *farangs* because they do not want their children following in their own footsteps. Generation after generation have had to work long hours in the sun in the rice paddies.

Our backs to the sky; our faces to the ground.

They want a better future for their children. If a temporary stint in the bars is the way to achieve that, then so be it.

A few girls do move up the social ladder in the sense that they now have money to spend and act as if they are members of high society. Money can get things done here but it will not change how you are perceived in the community. Marriage to a *farang* indicates you now have wealth but that is all it indicates.

Thais do not generally concern themselves with other people's business. They may not like hookers but there is no stigma or shame attached to what they do. Prostitutes may be snubbed socially but it will not be done overtly. And there will always be a smile.

Somporn was sitting with a Thai group of women while their western partners were having some beers together. Nevertheless, she was clearly outside their conversation. The smile was there and the social niceties were observed but she was not really regarded as being part of their group.

It is difficult for Westerners to pick up the subtle innuendos and body movements that show disdain and frostiness. We only see the smile and think all is well. It was not just how she was dressed – her tight-fitting short trousers and low-necked shirt were the "uniform" of the bargirl – it was the way she did not engage in the social chitchat with the other women. She also seemed to be avoiding eye contact.

There was no disgrace associated with the girl's background. That was not in question. She may not have been liked, but the reasons for her life style were understood. You could sense the distance that was being created between her and the others by the lack of friendly conversation. She was not completely fitting in.

We had decided to visit a farang friend living about one kilometre away and took two vehicles, one supposedly following the other. The first car drove off with Somporn and her boyfriend in the backseat. The second trailed behind very slowly. It never reached the friend's home.

What actually happened was that the female group in the second car had found a way of avoiding further contact with Somporn by "deliberately" getting lost. They had saved face by saying that they wanted to go but not turning up. They were making it clear, in the usual Thai indirect style, that they preferred their own company and social circle to being with a former bargirl.

She had not been accepted into their company.

Hopefully, *Sun, Sand, Sea, and Sex* has not only dispelled a few myths about Thailand's nightlife but has also put into perspective why the social and economic realities of Thailand have such an influence on Thai relationships throughout the country.

The next time you see the ladies of the night in Soi Bangla or Patpong ask yourself whether they have the radio on.

Chapter 9

All Thais Cheat

Thais can be a tad shy, keeping themselves to themselves, but they communicate well on important issues that involve the welfare of other people. Normally, when someone is gravely ill the "jungle drum" system of mobile phones and village gossip ensures everyone knows. But Lek, Stuart's wife, had not contacted friends when he had first been rushed to hospital and placed in intensive care. His pals were concerned for him and getting frustrated with her.

Lek was a former bargirl, and, although she was now caring for him 24/7 in an exemplary manner, there was a general suspicion amongst Stuart's friends that she wanted to ensure that her inheritance from him was not at risk of disappearing. They had known her a long time and she had always given the impression that she did not want his mates visiting him at home. It was something that Stuart was aware of but could do little about. He put a brave face on the situation. Stuart was in his late seventies, she was much younger.

She always dressed in short clothes. That left Thais in no doubt about her background. Westerners were less disapproving of how she dressed. It was not their business. They knew Stuart was being cared for, that was what mattered. But they were surprised when she had turned up at the hospital skimpily dressed.

He stayed in hospital for a week, the first two days in the IC unit. No one knew what was wrong. Was the hospital unsure or was she being reticent? He was discharged, given a great deal of medication, and told to rest at home. There was nothing more the hospital could do.

She hardly ever answered the phone when friends called, locked the gate, and would not answer the doorbell.

One of Stuart's newer western friends, a retired geriatric nurse called John, while in other ways helping a great deal, lost face, big time, by criticising some of Stuart's buddies. They had known him a long time and were aware of how protective she could be by not allowing his friends to visit. Not knowing Stuart and Lek that well, but trying to do his best for them in this situation, he completely failed to comprehend how saddened his old friends were at Lek's actions. John could have been more supportive by encouraging Lek to allow his friends to visit. It was what Stuart wanted. When Lek was not around, Stuart would phone his friends for a chat. But it was not the ideal state of affairs.

Farangs here can sometimes not be prepared to stand up to a Thai and girls like Lek know that, when their partner is elderly, they have the upper hand. The relationship can otherwise be a loving one and run smoothly most of the time.

Those that knew Stuart thought that there was a lack of trust between them. She was after his money and he had burned his boats and was making the best out of life in the circumstances. Thais do not trust easily. They are very cautious, even in dealings with their fellow countrymen.

Inter-family cheating is rare but not unknown when money is concerned. A relative may not be informed when someone is ill or dead. Unpleasantness develops when a family member will not release land deeds to the rightful owner. There are black sheep in all families of course. Cheating and corruption is endemic in Thai culture. We shall look later at why this may be the case.

Cars had parked very closely to me. I had little space to manoeuvre. My wing mirror slightly touched another car but I checked that there was no damage to either vehicle. This was at Wat Phra Dhammakaya, on the outskirts of Bangkok, and I was moving my car to another part of the complex to visit some friends.

On leaving their apartment two hours later, I saw a crowd, including a security guard, hovering over the two cars. They said that I had damaged another vehicle and pointed to several areas on the rear and offside bodywork. The security guard said he had seen the damage being caused. I had seen his being slipped two 100-baht notes.

The insurance assessor was trying to find a compromise and a money sum that would settle the matter. Establishing fault did not seem to be a priority. Avoiding a row and not spending too much time talking appeared to be their solution. If the *farang* has more money than the Thai does, then the *farang* pays. I think that was my assessor's logic too.

Compromising when there is some doubt on liability would be reasonable. But why should I give way when the guard had been so blatantly bribed? There was rust on some of the alleged damage. That would not have formed in the short time I had been at the *wat*, whether I had damaged all four sides of his car or not.

I made it clear that I was not going to accept being at fault. There was no recent damage to either vehicle. My insurance assessor realised I was not going to give in.

I was being asked to fund some repairs the other person needed on his car. He still wanted some sort of settlement and the usual haggling started. *Farangs* have been known to give way in minor disputes like this. They don't want the hassle, particularly when another language is involved. Most Thais are reasonable but some are unscrupulous and will try to make a profit from the situation.

Tongue in cheek, I took the Thai stance of suggesting that the police attend and make a report. In Thailand, the police have almost court-like powers. Arguing or explaining your version of events is not usually an option, especially if you are *farang*.

If I were Thai, the police officer would have seen the rust and may have dismissed the case. But I knew that he might not have taken such a view with a *farang*. An officer can sometimes not see things clearly when expats are involved. Even amongst Thais, a police officer would usually favour a motor cyclist against a motorist if there were an accident. He is more likely to be a rider than a car driver himself and so would be more sympathetic to the rider's position. As the rider may be uninsured and have little money, he would take the practical and realistic view that the motorist is at fault and his insurance company can pay. That would not be western logic.

Then a monk walked by. Apparently, he recognised me as a student in one of his meditation classes and said so. The occupants of the car I had allegedly damaged were coming to visit him at the temple. He was their son.

The quibbling farce went on. The monk remained quiet. I told my assessor to deal with it. I was handling it the Thai way. I had not accused anyone of cheating. I had not raised my voice. I was not smiling as a Thai would have been, but neither was I getting angry.

After calmly explaining again that I did not cause the damage, I pointed to the rust. Although I did not openly say so, they seemed well aware that I had observed the 200-baht being handed over. They stopped arguing but kept on smiling. I smiled too and drove off.

Paraphrasing the American poet Adrienne Rich: *Lying is not only done with words but also with silence.*

No doubt, the insurance company filed their papers. I heard no more from them. The monk's parents are still probably driving around in a vehicle with rust damage on all four sides. The monk is, I am sure, still teaching meditation.

The two examples of Lek and the monk's family show how cheating can be part of the Thai way of thinking. Thais come from a background of poverty and the idea of survival of the fittest is born of necessity. The gap between rich and poor is wide. At one extreme the wealth of the richest family business in Thailand equates to 5% of the country's gross domestic product; on the other, families are living on less than 300 baht a day.

A Thai lady lost a valuable watch in a shopping precinct in the UK. Passers by, sensing something was amiss, asked what was bothering her. They suggested contacting the local police station. She was visibly taken aback by what she thought was an absurd suggestion. Most Thais would keep something valuable if they found it. She would have done so herself. And surely the police would not admit to receiving lost property anyway. Thinking it would be a waste of time, she did, however, go to the station. Someone had picked up the watch, taken it to the police, and she was able to reclaim her watch. Even then, she thought she would have to pay some money to the officers for their help. Back in Thailand, she may have reverted to type. She had admitted that she herself would have kept a watch if she found one. Such instincts may be hard to lose.

Foreigners, and particularly tourists, will be over-charged in most countries. In Thailand, such price discrimination is in theory illegal but is widespread even in state-owned businesses such as national parks, museums, and other attractions.

Usually Arabic (1,2,3,4...) and not Thai numerals (which look like squiggles to western eyes) are shown in displaying prices throughout Thailand. Some government documents use Thai numerals but they are not generally used in normal commerce. If you see both Arabic and Thai numbers on price information boards you can be sure that the Thai figures do not correspond with the prices shown in the English translation. The Thai price will always be less, sometimes up to a tenth of the *farang* price. The intention is to cheat.

The argument that it is fair because *farangs* do not always pay Thai taxes or are richer than Thais is phony. The Thai occupants of a top of the range Mercedes would pay the same lower price on entering a national park as any other Thai. Having a two-tier pricing structure in place is simply a means of taking advantage of the foreigner. The high flows of foreign reserves into Thailand most years make discriminatory pricing unnecessary from an economics viewpoint anyway. It simply comes down to cheating the foreigner.

The employees at the ticket booths are noticeably embarrassed when the discriminatory prices are pointed out. They dislike the practice but are bound by the rules. Showing a Thai driving licence or engaging in some small talk, cracking a joke maybe, can help. It allows them to think of a way to accept charging you the Thai price without losing face.

As in many countries, saying a few words like hello and thank you in the host language can work to your benefit and is very much appreciated by Thais.

A Thai policeman stops a *farang* whom he sees leaving a bar and riding his motorbike towards him. The foreigner is not wearing his safety helmet. It is stowed, as is usual in Thailand, in the front basket.

400 baht please, he says.

Oh, come on, officer. I only live down this soi. My riding's okay, isn't it? You've seen me safely ride down this road from the bar every evening this week. And all Thais ride after a few drinks.

That cut no ice with the officer.

Perfect riding, sir. I look at it differently. I've watched you drinking in that bar. You have spent more in the last few hours than I earn in three days.

Think of the 400 baht as part of my salary. It is not an unreasonable sum compared with the salaries paid to western police forces. I'm doing my job just as they are. We all need to be rewarded for our work, whatever job we do. It is just that eastern countries have a different sort of payment system.

There have been some serious banking and financial services scandals in the West in recent years that suggest we should be careful how we criticise Thailand and other developing nations on matters of cheating and corruption. HSBC was fined almost 2 billion dollars by US regulators for their connection with Afghan drug barons in late 2012. No prosecutions were brought. No senior employee was fired. Salaries and bonuses remained high. Thais can point to that when they themselves are condemned for corrupt activities. They see that it is, on the face of it, acceptable in western culture. Confidence tricksters are of many different nationalities.

Corruption is rife in countries of the Far East, Thailand being no exception. It is part of their culture and the practice is very often transparent and accepted. They think of it as a normal part of their daily earnings. It makes no difference whether it is a few hundred baht to process a transaction more quickly or a sweetener of several million to secure a contract.

There are expat residents who have perpetrated serious property and financial scams in Thailand. A bankrupt double glazing businessman and an ex Tupperware salesman have been exposed in the Thai press for alleged property fraud. Their confidence tricks succeed because many *farangs* do not know Thai law and trust English speaking fellow expats to navigate them through the maze. These fraudsters cleverly ingratiate themselves into local organisations, claim impressive qualifications, appear to be well recommended, and socialise with high-ranking Thais. All to provide a cover of respectability in order to keep their business methods out of the limelight.

They engage in photo opportunities with high-level officials whenever they can. *Farangs* may be led to believe this gives them a stamp of approval of their activities from the authorities. Nothing can be further from the truth. The officers may have no involvement or knowledge of what they are up to.

Understanding how one can get things done quite legally and easily here is the answer. By seeking out professionals and getting guidance from the ordinary honest Thai, you can steer clear of the more dangerous and costly rip-offs, whether by Thais or *farangs*. Relying on people only because they speak good English means you are limiting your choice in selecting those who can give you good advice. It is not compulsory to deal only with advisors who speak English.

The locals, if you get to know them and have a rapport, are usually good sources of information and will recommend people that are more reliable. When I first came to Thailand, I was told: "Get to know your Thai." I assumed I was being advised to improve my language skills. But no, my mentor was referring to my sizing up the Thai people before dealing with them. Even in hailing a *tuk tuk* he would look at the driver's face before deciding to get in. If Thais do that, so should we. As he said, "Sometimes, I am embarrassed by my fellow countrymen."

Foreign owners of condominiums can be elected to the juristic committee in charge of the condo and vote to circumvent the very restrictive and expensive clauses that are often found in property maintenance contracts. The Thais routinely get rid of the initial committee and run it themselves. Expats could do the same.

What permeates through the social structure of Thailand is the forbearance of petty cheating. Cases where money is extorted are more clearly visible here, much more out in the open. This is very true of developing countries where the majority of the population remains relatively poor. It is widespread and endemic in this country and in other eastern cultures. For smaller amounts, "under the counter" payments are actually handed over in full view of everyone. A transparency that is par for the course in Thailand.

A large private company was experiencing increasing fraud and thefts. Controls were quickly established when the new chairman, Tongchai, took over. The most serious swindles stopped.

As happens when the reins are held more tightly, smaller transgressions are discovered. The director responsible for transport had been generously lining his own pocket by fiddling expenses. Daily running costs of his family's cars were being charged to the company fleet. He was a long-serving director and everyone thought he was beyond reproach.

A new system set up to monitor vehicle mileage showed his official company vehicle was only averaging 3 kilometres per litre. Obviously, not all the fuel was going into the one tank. It was amazing how many new tyres were being bought for his car. He had concealed these activities for over a decade.

The owner of the company was informed.

Do you think I don't know what's been going on? You know how much we pay him and even adding on these perks we are still getting a good deal for the work he does. The suppliers only give him what has been agreed with me in any case.

Quoting from the Roman scholar, Petronius, Tongchai's final words were, *Mundus vult decipi; decipiatur*. The world wants to be cheated, so cheat.

Take your car for a service and be prepared to watch while they work on your car. They won't object since that is what Thais would do. Most service centres have a mezzanine floor where you see most of what is going on. Ask them to give you the packaging for any new parts that they fit and the return of the used parts. They won't find such requests unusual. You would probably be met with a storm of protest if you tried that in the West. But Thais accept that trust is in short supply in their country.

Slip out for a quick coffee and you may miraculously find on your return that they've finished with your car and carried out all the required jobs! I told a Thai businessman once that I thought he was devious. He actually took it as a compliment. I learnt much from that.

So, do all Thais cheat?

Reading comments on some of the forums or listening to people holding forth in a bar after having one over the eight, one might well think so.

I know a man that lost everything: house, car, his savings, everything. I know hundreds if not thousands of expats like him. I tell you. They all cheat. It's in the blood.

Yes, it happens, but the anecdotes often get exaggerated and like most stories, there are usually two sides to them. Taxi drivers may try to fix the meter so that it records a higher fare. But then there are verified instances where a driver, finding a wallet or other valuables in the back of his cab, spends an hour tracking down his customer and returning them.

Thai internet forums can be variable in the quality and accuracy of their information. Sometimes the advice can be helpful and useful; sometimes, totally misleading. It is worthwhile reading forums occasionally to get a different, though maybe one-sided, view of Thailand. A more balanced source of information is http://www.andrew-drummond.com. Drummond is a western journalist who has spent a great deal of time in Thailand and is an ardent campaigner on concerns that *farangs* have in their daily lives here. His style can be a little sensationalist – he was a former News of the World reporter – but many expats have good reason to be grateful for his efforts.

(Ctrl and click will generally work or you can type in the link above into your internet browser window.)

It is always wise to be cautious in a foreign country. The perfectly spoken gentleman with a clipped Oxford accent may well be a tout for a gem fraud or an overpriced tourist attraction. He is out to win your confidence and then cheat you.

I have overheard Thai women, speaking in Thai to a vendor, organising special commissions for themselves while supposedly negotiating for the best price for their husband or boyfriend.

Petty corruption is not in practice a crime here. It has always been a part of Thai life. Westerners think of it differently. They see all corruption as wrong. Look out for yourself in Thailand on all money transactions. They check every business detail and watch body language. Maybe we should too.

Legal disputes are settled by reference to written or photographic evidence. Thais are aware of the value of taking photographs as proof of what actually happened and in an attempt to stop things going further. A lorry had entered the driveway of the house next door to make it easier to offload some sand and cement onto the adjoining property. Within minutes, neighbours were taking photographs as a precaution in case any damage was caused and legal action needed to be taken.

Case law is seldom brought up in Thai courts and is given little weight. There is no jury system in Thailand where your peers try you. Judges are bound by what is prescribed by the legislation. While Thais may be both gainers and losers in the system, *farangs* more often than not only lose.

Giving money under the counter gets things done more quickly. Thais find nothing unusual in this. Procedures are completed less problematically and it is the way it has been done for centuries. As a *farang*, try to see the situation with those same Thai eyes. Smile; speak a few words of Thai. The situation will become more comfortable if you do things the Thai way, however unlike carrying out similar transactions may be in the West.

What would be your choice? Paying 2000 baht at your embassy for a confirmation of address and obtaining a receipt, or openly slipping a 500-baht note to a Thai government official. The money is shared among the staff and is a time-honoured perquisite, in practice part of the salary. It helps the applicant, it helps the employee, and is completely transparent. It harms no one and this sort of openness is not regarded as corruption.

A Thai man gets into a sawngtaew (two-bench open pick up truck,) and agrees his 30-baht fare expecting to be taken to his destination. A rather well heeled tourist then hails the cab and offers 300 baht for the driver to take him to a travel agent straightaway, wait for him there, and bring him back home. The deal is a good one for the driver and he asks the first passenger to get out.

Technically, the passenger can insist on the driver carrying out his part of the bargain but he knows that the police, if called, would side with the cabbie. Accepting a more lucrative fare is a good business deal for the driver. Principles do not enter into it.

The average Thai knows he has to leave the cab and would have sympathised with the driver's reasoning and business acumen. If the first passenger had been a middle class Thai the result might have been a little different. The driver would have quietly taken him nearer to his destination before driving at speed to the travel agents with his new fare.

Coming back from a tourist attraction, a visitor may be dropped off at another venue and not at his hotel. Or, if the taxi driver is about to start his daily school run, he may decline to take you further. You may be asked to get out, wait, and hail another cab. We would find that strange and unfair. The Thais do not. To them, it is reasonable that the school contract has precedence. They don't mind the inconvenience of getting another taxi. To the Thai, it is another instance of *Mai bpen rai*. To argue would result in loss of face, so they won't do that either. Many cultural beliefs inter-relate in Thailand.

A small mama and papa shop may have to pay a small bribe to have some protection. It is seen as an unavoidable overhead to which the shopkeeper has to agree. If a richer Thai or a *farang* comes along later, he can always charge a little more to cover the cost of the bribe. It is a common feature in eastern countries. The payment is justified as a form of gift. It originates from the Thai belief in *sin nam jai*, gifts to high officials.

Petty corruption is not only a Thai phenomenon. A shopkeeper in a small village in the UK opened her shop every day of the week for the convenience of her customers. It was in the days when opening on the Sabbath was discouraged and it was illegal to sell certain products. certain an area where Sunday opening was discouraged and, for some items, sales were illegal on the Sabbath. The local policeman would always pop in to say hello while on his morning stroll round his patch. He always came away with something, some bars of chocolate for his children maybe. It relieved the boredom of plodding his beat. It doesn't happen now in the UK of course. Police officers no longer plod beats; they sit behind desks.

Sometimes it's best to turn a blind eye, Pranom said to the new English teacher.

But Mana was blatantly cheating and he knew that I'd seen him leaning over and copying from the friend next to him. How can you condone that, Pranom?

I too wish the cheating had not occurred but Mana's parents saved hard to pay for his education at this university. It is a step up for them and they feel it gives them merit that their son is being given opportunities that they did not have themselves. Mana will lose face. The parents will lose face. You'll find it difficult to continue teaching in that class. I don't want to lose you but I would have to transfer you to another department. Westerners don't always appreciate the Thai sensitivity to loss of face and its effect on a person's friends or colleagues. So, should we avoid conflict and loss of face for everyone and forget it.

Yes, okay, but it's not the way we would have handled it in the West, Pranom.

As I am writing this a good example of cheating occurred. A local plumber who had been doing some repairs in the house decided to help himself to some fuel for his motor bike. He lived some distance away and I frequently put some petrol in his tank. Today, when I was not looking, he filled the tank to the brim. With diesel! He had picked up the wrong can of fuel.

He spent the afternoon emptying the tank and flushing through the system. By convention, he still gets paid for a full day's work and would not think of replenishing the fuel he took. I get less frustrated and annoyed at incidents such as these now. The best advice I can offer is to be aware that these aggravations can happen. As Westerners, we will never completely understand this mindset.

According to recent figures on corruption in South East Asia, Thailand ranks as being more corrupt than Malaysia but less corrupt than the Philippines, Indonesia, Vietnam, Cambodia, Laos, and Myanmar.

One of Thailand's Asean partners, Singapore, has the reputation of being the least dishonest country in South East Asia and the third least corrupt in the world.

It has a zero tolerance for sleaze and the laws do not differentiate between rich and poor. The big bosses who control the frauds are punished along with those directly collecting the bribes.

That was not always the state of affairs. Although the 1871 Penal Code of the Straits Settlements, enacted four years after Singapore was colonised, made corruption illegal; the British in reality did little or nothing to stop it. Throughout the 1880s, police corruption was widespread. Even the December 1937 anti-corruption law was not strong enough. During the Japanese occupation (1942 – 1945) high inflation meant corruption also spread to the civil service as employees were seeing the real value of their salaries diminish. The problem was tackled only after the war, when Singaporeans were increasingly given more power to conduct their own affairs. It was then that the legislation got tougher and was enforced.

Since independence in August 1965, Singapore increased its fight against cheating and bribery. There appeared to be a political determination to end corruption at all levels; to enact and put into effect robust legislation; and to increase salaries to a point where the personal need for engaging in graft or sleaze was minimised.

Political will and a real demand for change from the people seem to be the keys that are needed for change. It happened in Singapore, it could eventually happen here if salaries became more in line with the cost of living. Low salaries allow corruption to take hold.

In today's Thailand, the answer to petty corruption is, sadly, to say *mai bpen rai* and accept it, possibly justifying not taking further action by believing the perpetrators will be punished for their bad karma in the next life. No need to get involved now. Let it be. The Thais call money corruptly received *satang rawn*, (hot money) but that is as far as they will acknowledge the problem.

Cheating and corruption are not regarded as totally wrong in Thailand. They permit the wheels to turn smoothly. If a person has become rich through corrupt practice then perhaps it is a karmic reward for past good deeds. Is the logic of karma sanctioning corruption? It is possibly compensation for past conduct in much the same way as bribes and under the counter payments are today considered part of people's wage and salaries.

Sin nam jai, the giving of a gift as a bribe or a goodwill payment, is commonplace. The Italians have similar expressions: *you should let me dip my beak and draw water from your well.* Many societies sense a need to conform to what are generally established norms within their communities..

The Thais in the old days used to have an expression, *kin meuang,* when applied to the state taking a percentage off the top of a business transaction. Literally, it meant, *eating the state*. This was part of the Thai *khunnang* system that allowed some of the élite to get kickbacks from money collected from the local populace, whether by means of taxes or other payments levied.

Today, something similar happens. There are usually no formal requests for such payments. It is considered wise to offer a gift voluntarily. If an official makes any suggestion, it is couched in terms such as "We need to make a small cash charge to cover our admin costs." This "tea money" is not that much different from the example of the UK shopkeeper quoted earlier. All forms of corruption have an eventual cost. It is built into the price the end user pays.

The commissions and kickbacks paid by large corporations in the West to secure business are cases in point. The truth is that people think of many of the world's top businessmen as taking advantage of their positions of trust. American and British banks came under scrutiny for very dubious dealings, both domestically and internationally, in the early part of the twenty-first century. Money laundering and rate fixing effectively went unpunished The small fines imposed were paid for from higher charges to customers. No one served jail time nor lost any sleep when it was clear some of the money laundering operations involved drug barons in Afghanistan. Meetings to consider the level of bonuses to bankers were seen as more important than considering how many lives were lost as a result of the drug barons illegal activities that the banks had facilitated.

In late 2013 there was a crash landing at the main airport in Bangkok that hit world headlines. A substandard runway was blamed. The consensus, though, was that corruption in contract tendering had resulted in corners being cut in the original construction work. A spate of train derailments occurred at around the same time. Whether due to corruption or lack of finance for maintenance was never established.

The hierarchical system in Thailand means that the lower levels of society are neither keen nor confident in challenging the networks about their unfair and corrupt practices. We are not doing an effective job of it in the West; it would be even more difficult in the East where there are cultural reasons for keeping the status quo.

A developing modern education system may eventually encourage some change from the more natural Thai instinct of accepting things as they are. It will be a slow process. Education is never a high priority anywhere in the world. East or West. And it is only a better-educated populace that will bring about gradual change.

The opposition to holding elections through the ballot box in February 2014 showed that a large majority of the population of Thailand had no understanding of the concept of democracy. There was much talk and propaganda about alleged corruption by the current government led by Yingluck Shiniwatra, the sister of former Prime Minister Thaksin who had been exiled following the 2006 coup.

Corruption and misdeeds by other political parties were not so widely publicised in the media. Higher education standards in Thailand may have made people challenge some of the biased reporting and made them think about the real issues of what democracy and the right of a universal vote is about. One elderly lady existing on a few hundred baht monthly pension voted against the government even though it was that party that gave her affordable healthcare and other benefits. She could see no link between her vote and the benefits promised by a political party in a manifesto. The basic principle of her having a say in government escaped her. She wanted the country to be governed by the unelected "great and the good" to whom she had always been taught to respect.

The National Anti-Corruption Commission, and other government departments, NGOs and the judiciary, have some influence in combating corruption but the established and ingrained values of most Thais are an even more powerful force. Those ideals are changing but changing only little by little. Each successive generation of Thais, keen to see higher and fairer wages in an economically richer, stable, and democratic country will carry that development further. The more the press is free; the more new ideas will be aired.

The maxim quoted by Tongchai, *Mundus vult decipi; decipiatur. The world wants to cheat; so cheat,* may get less relevant but I doubt we have seen its complete demise.

Chapter 10

The Thai Mafia

Every country has organised crime syndicates operating within its borders. With its powerful mafia families, Thailand is no exception.

Whether it is called Mafia, Triads, Camorra, or Yakuza; organised crime has existed for centuries and continues to flourish throughout the world. By whatever name, these businesses – for that is what they really are – set themselves apart from other organisations by having a philosophy that their power in society is absolute. They owe no allegiance to governments or countries. They believe that they create real power by being secretive and creating loyalty amongst their members. Ingratiating themselves with useful officials is a common tactic that is usually accompanied by bribes as an inducement to comply with their wishes. Once on side, it may be difficult for such people to be anything other than very cooperative. So blind eyes are turned.

Mafias operate through legitimate companies and, despite what is popularly thought, their business activities range more widely than drugs, prostitution, gambling, arms smuggling, protection rackets, and human trafficking. Their fingers are in many pies. They have influence in some very large businesses and, it is claimed, in government departments.

They are the same as all other organisations. They have boards of directors; they have finance, marketing, and human resources departments. No business can run without some sort of formality and structure. Mafias are not dissimilar. The difference is that the bosses admit to no supreme authority other than their own. Their loyalty is to their extended family of members and not to any legal or moral code.

The companies become valuable covers for illegal operations such as loan sharking and black market trading. The huge cash flow that is generated, both internally in Thailand and from abroad, helps the national economy, employment levels grow, and the reserves of foreign currency are increased. Although the cash is lost to the state as there is no tax revenue, it is not lost to the economy. It can and is used to generate business growth, albeit within a limited circle. But the economy itself does not suffer other than in the creation of a more monopolistic structure that is not conducive to fair competition. There are plenty of businesses that do not trade fairly. It is not the prerogative of organised crime syndicates.

In Thailand, as elsewhere, some of the profits are channeled towards social welfare projects, (which are controlled by the mafia families and not the state) and to charitable foundations in the community. Large corporations associate themselves with agricultural and environmental projects, the *wats* receive large donations from the élite as well as the money given as merit from ordinary Thais. Local communities benefit from their generosity.

At times, the large volume of cash accumulated by the Mafias can result in the manipulation of stock and currency markets, the latter particularly in times of Baht volatility.

The Italian concept of *omertà*, the code of honour forbidding the disclosure of information to outsiders and non-cooperation with the authorities, is effective in societies such as Thailand's where, as we have seen, it is instinctive for people to be dedicated to family or an élite rather than the state. Thais feel an obligation to those higher up the social hierarchy. Such feudal ideas are difficult for the Thais to shake off. This allegiance is more of a cultural force than an attribute of "loyalty." They are values that are regarded as more important than adhering to any system of law and order dictated by any government. The Thai's definition of freedom is to obey the moral and societal rules of family and community.

Thais do not normally get involved in other people's affairs. *Tura mai chai* (it's not my problem) ensures that they do not talk out of turn about matters that are private to themselves or their group. They are cautious of people with outward signs of wealth and power, but, if they do get involved, treat them with the utmost respect.

Mafias – and there is no such entity as a single mafia – obtain allegiance within the "family" by always looking after its members financially and socially. Provided that they continue to be guarded about the organisation and do not cooperate with any law enforcement or justice agency in any action against them, they will always be secure in the community of that "family" for the rest of their lives. The need for financial security is essential to a Thai household. So, such a promise is not taken lightly.

Thais are fond of social networks and need to be part of cliques. According to Jane Bunnag, they tend not to cooperate outside those sets to which they have decided to belong. Thais are individualistic and dislike competition. The protection and safety they get from being amongst other people in those social groups is a powerful need, whether that is in the camaraderie of the workplace or neighbourhood, or in the membership of like-minded people. The model of Thailand's strong family and community culture is practically purpose-built for a mafia organisation. Thais like the security of a group controlled by a strong and respected leader and the protection it provides. They respect a father figure, whether that is someone they see as an official leader or someone reputed to be a mafiosi. Belonging to a syndicate or belonging to the local community run by your *puyaibaan* have powerful paybacks for the Thai. Both offer the key need a Thai has for wellbeing and security. They know they will get unreserved support and protection from the *naklaeng dto* or gang leaders when it is needed.

In the late nineteenth century, Thailand saw the emergence of the *Angyee* criminal gangs, as secret and feared as any modern day *cosa nostra*. They became prominent in many business sectors. Although the Thai Criminal Code prohibited membership of this and similar criminal groups, the law had limited success in enforcement because of the covert nature of the gangs and their power in society.

Kung Sa was a crime association that originated in Myanmar and controlled drug operations. The principal chieftains were arrested by the Thai authorities and handed over to the Americans for prosecution. Kung Sa's businesses were later reinstated under a group called The United Wa State Army and continued to sell drugs within Thailand.

Present day godfathers are called *poo mee itthipon* or *kon mee itthipon* (literally; person with influence) and still carry on the traditions inherent in all mafia activities. Any title in Thai preceded by the word *poo* shows that the person is one to be respected in society. Judges, for example, are called *poo peepaksa* – in public at least.

The use if the word *poo* – despite its unfortunate connotations to the western ear – is further evidence of the respectful subservience given to those seen as being in high positions in Thailand. Most countries would call them criminals or gangsters. Thais elevate them to the status of *poo mee itthipon*.

The precise words used in the language very often give a potent insight into the way the Thai thinks. The frequent use of *krap, ka,* and *krapom* at the end of most sentences in a conversation is a good illustration of how a Thai believes in and reinforces class differences between himself and the person being spoken to.

As a last resort, assassinations may take place when there is non-compliance with the organisation's wishes and the bosses feel a loss of face and respect. Given how key these two notions are to

Thais, one can readily see how mafias get a hold in this country. It is not only a matter of power and money.

The mobs solutions to problems they encounter in their businesses are not always instantaneous. They give the impression of being well timed and well planned. They are subtle, effective, and give a clear message. There may be violence but there is also a sense that social justice, not available from the authorities, has been done. The neighbourhood does not forget that law and order has been delivered in this way.

It is a Thai characteristic to repay favours when someone helps you makes your life safe and secure. The local *poo mee itthipon* can fulfill that role. He may be in a monopolistic sort of business, he may be rich and used to getting his own way, but if he is seen to be giving security to the community, then the downsides of his activities are outweighed by the benefits he offers.

Many frauds against tourists and *farangs* are operated by Mafia gangs. Though "gangs" is not the most appropriate word for well-dressed men and women with impeccable manners and polished accents. Although the smaller and less powerful syndicates are active in this area, the larger mafias do have a stake in the more lucrative and complex frauds involving land and business deals.

Thais do not deal directly with problems head on. They are more likely to walk away and respond later in a different manner. They are not turning the other cheek, quite the opposite. It is natural for them to use an intermediary to intervene when they would feel uncomfortable to negotiate or get drawn in themselves. Mafias find that Thai trait effective in their own operations. The leaders are not seen to be personally connected with the dispute.

Using go-betweens to avoid conflict is a common Thai trait. More common than in the West where contact is more direct and transparent. For instance, marriage negotiations may involve an intermediary, the *mae sue*, to act for both potential marriage partners. Mafias use intermediaries too. They use "buffers" to prevent any links being established between the main bosses who control the business and give the orders, and those who carry them out. Arrests and prosecutions are unlikely when there is no direct evidence of any wrongdoing being traced to them.

Mafias benefit from their status and position in the Thai hierarchy in order to bid for business contracts in a way that ensures that their rivals are reluctant to tender. A suggestion that they wish to be the sole bidder is usually sufficient to eliminate any competition.

"Tea money" is collected to allow individuals or businesses to operate under mafia protection. These syndicates provide a vigilante force to guarantee no trouble and smooth business operations. Regular rents or commissions are collected as a percentage of profits or turnover. Thailand is very much a money culture. Money talks. It gets things done. Residents of *moobaans* and owners of department stores will employ, and pay for, their own security services. Private enterprise is preferred to relying on the state police force. The old western idea of trusting and seeking help from the bobby on the beat would seem incredibly naive to a Thai and it is therefore unlikely that the public would offer them any assistance or support in return. Rarely if ever do Thais collaborate or help the police. They look to people of influence or social standing to deal with problems.

One of the difficulties in controlling and prosecuting mafia crime is that it often operates internationally. Because they act in secret and are difficult to trace, crime syndicates can be confident that there will be little or no enforcement from the police and justice system.

Although there is legislation against narcotics, human trafficking, and money laundering; there is no overall coordinated legislation covering all mafia businesses. Each crime is dealt with solely under legislation relevant to that offence. That was particularly true prior to 2004. In a trial on drugs handling the evidence of linked offences such as money laundering and conspiracy cannot be heard.

The National Counter Corruption Commission (NCCC), which was set up following the 1975 Prevention and Suppression of Corruption Act, is as strong as it can be. All the same, it cannot act against people believed to be members of an organized crime syndicate when the bosses cannot be located or named and no real proof of their involvement can be produced. That is a worldwide difficulty.

Freemasonry is full of secret words and gestures. Belonging to some sort of clandestine brotherhood has its attractions for many people. Signs and expressions are used to find out whether the person you are speaking to is a member of a mafia group or a freemasonry lodge. If a mason asks you if you are a cautious man, the form of words you use in reply will tell him if you too are a mason. He would never ask directly. Mafias probably use something similar.

Some ordinary Thais are drawn to the activities of these mafias. There is a certain glamour about syndicate membership. Being linked to influential people or the élite is appealing to the Thai as it can outwardly show their status. It is natural for Thais to show their class and position by uniforms, insignia, and the way they dress and behave. Appearance is all-important to them as they feel a need to confirm their place in society. Although Mafiosi don't wear uniforms, they show their position by their confident behaviour. Giving the impression that you belong to a mafia has a certain appeal to some Thais, an appeal that the mafia families benefit from.

Some claims of involvement are likely to be tales of fiction with little or no substance. Even expats allege close friendship with senior police or government officials. It is not a uniquely Thai peculiarity. People who are actually drawn in to the groups, particularly at senior level, don't brag about or advertise their connections. Society knows who the gang members are, they don't need to be reminded.

Mafia members come from varying backgrounds and are of different nationalities. It is certainly not true that they are all Thai. Establishing prostitution rings outside Thailand and the trafficking of cheap labour from bordering countries are two prime examples of how these crimes are multi-national.

The Thai writer, Wanchai Roujanavong, discusses his ideas on money laundering, corruption, and changes in defamation legislation that could improve the current success rate against the mafia bosses. He advocates more international cooperation, tougher rules preventing membership of illegal syndicates, more forceful measures to counteract obstruction to justice, and tighter controls to stop witness intimidation.

All countries, including Thailand, that are signatories to the United Nations Conventions against Transnational Organised Crime agree to follow the conventions "in a manner consistent with the principles of sovereign ... and territorial integrity." The conventions are not laws and each country can interpret the agreements according to its own cultural and legal systems. Thais want to avoid altercations and not create waves. They have a disproportionate respect for those with money, wealth, and power. Their instinct for *mai bpen rai* is dominant. Such a combination is not helpful when the state is up against the mafias. There is too much of a *not my problem, nothing to do with me* attitude.

Thailand passed the Money Laundering Control Act in 1999, but this and other rulings are seen as weaker in their scope than those of other countries, notably Australia and Malaysia. Much of the Thai legislation is linked to specific crimes. Nothing outside those offences can technically be investigated. This played into the hands of the mobs. The 2004 Special Case Investigation Act was a positive step forward in plugging this loophole, but it has not completely achieved its goal.

Justice would be better served if, for example, it were possible for a case of human trafficking to be dealt with by bringing in the links to prostitution and money laundering. Easier to get a conviction if all aspects could be investigated in the same trial instead of only one indictment being heard.

The use of agent provocateurs by the police and other enforcement agencies can be challenged by defence lawyers if the relevant statute is not precisely followed. The setting up of controlled deliveries; for example of drugs, weapons, or human traffic, could be considered as breaking the law. Those working undercover would have no protection against prosecution. Telephone tapping and computer surveillance need careful authorisation to circumvent a challenge in court. During legal proceedings, it often looks as if the mafias have been dealt all the trump cards. They constantly come out on top of the game.

The Thai justice system rightly holds great store in trying to protect the individual from the power of the state. The consequent weakness is that there is more concern about the rules of evidence and the presumption of innocence than neutralising well-known members of the mob. Every country faces the same problem of balancing people's freedoms with strong laws and practices aimed at weakening organised crime. The extra-judicial killings in the 2003 anti-drug wars in Thailand took out many gangsters but also resulted in innocent people being killed.

The will to change and get the balance right may be there, but it will be a sluggish process.

Getting hard evidence is always complicated in prosecuting for money laundering, as the paper trails are rarely transparent, particularly if the use of overseas bank accounts makes obtaining proof difficult. It does not help that no individual prosecutions were ever brought against one of the world's biggest banks when it admitted money laundering in drug networks. In December 2012, HSBC were fined but continued to operate; hardly a good western rôle model for persuading developing countries to effectively enforce laws against the mafia.

Whistle blowing and getting details from informants are not common or acceptable characteristics of the Thai. They mind their own business and are a bit uncertain of the police. Both the constitution and other acts of parliament provide for witness protection, but manpower costs can prove prohibitive if security is necessary for long periods after any trial is over. Most Thais would consider carefully whether to cooperate or not. *Omertà* would probably be their choice. When witnesses are brought to court, attempts are made to provide anonymity so that lives are not put in danger. Most people would probably remain unconvinced of such promises, believing that the mob's influence would more than counteract any guarantee of safety by the authorities.

Punishments for libel and slander are severe in Thailand. Damaging a person's reputation or business, even by just naming and shaming with your personal honest opinion, is illegal. Truth is not a defence. Loss of face trumps telling the truth every time. People think twice about making accusations because of this interpretation and definition of libel and slander.

Efforts are continually being made to combat corruption through the National Counter Corruption Commission. Its focus, however, is on individual cases rather than on large-scale group involvement. Therefore, repeatedly, the big boys at the top escape justice.

You will see routine police checkpoints on the major roads into the country and officers regularly visit construction sites to detain prohibited foreign workers. It is more difficult though to apprehend those who are actually running the illegal labour schemes. They are never in the public eye.

Cheap immigrant labour, trafficked into Thailand by these organised gangs, keeps their profits up. The economy can appear to be growing, with workers productively engaged. However, businesses that try to operate legally are at a disadvantage when competing with the mafias with their cheap source of manpower.

Organised crime is involved in arms smuggling with some south east Asian countries being acknowledged as the centre. But nothing ever gets proven.

The larger and more dominant mafias are prolific recruiting grounds for pork-barrel politics where politicians can obtain favours for their particular constituencies and avoid the checks and balances of strict democracy. Wanchai quotes the Klom Dan Waste Water Treatment Plant where 23 billion baht disappeared because people were pulling strings. Of course, Thailand is not alone in this form of business strategy.

Some special powers have been given in law to minimise bail skipping and intimidation but a strong international agency dedicated to fighting organised crime is what is really needed. Mobsters benefit from weak extradition treaties and a less than perfect global communication system between enforcement agencies.

Though not talking specifically about Thailand, Senator Robert Kennedy said in 1960, during America's most fierce attack on the mafias, "If we do not attack organised criminals with weapons and techniques as effective as their own, they will destroy us."

Sovereign states are trying to find ways around the strict letter of the law in order to combat the activities of organised gangs and to get on a more level playing field. Countries are restricted by their laws; the gangs have a freer hand. Mafias don't operate under the restrictions that a system of checks and balances forces on government law officers. Although Thai judges have inquisitorial powers and can ask witnesses questions, they are properly reluctant to do so as they do not wish to be seen to be favouring one side or the other in a case. Prosecuting barristers are not as tough as their western counterparts are when it comes to attacking a defendant's testimony. Thais dislike conflict, argument, and losing face. It is instructive to watch a court case in Thailand and compare it with the western equivalent.

In the past, Thailand has confiscated the proceeds of crime where maybe the evidence may technically not have been strong enough. Pragmatic measures are sometimes justified. Under UN conventions, it is legally possible to extract compensation from wrongdoers. But in some instances, the funds have to go to sovereign state treasuries as determined by international law rather than to actual victims.

Organised crime members can act quickly and are not bothered about the need for strict rules of evidence and search warrants. Governments and agencies seeking to improve enforcement need to keep ahead of the game if they are to compete in winning this global war. The belief that some people are beyond the scope of law needs to be addressed.

Thais find access to the justice system expensive and bureaucratic. They distrust it and do not see it as particularly effective or fair. They know successful judgments against the mafias are difficult to obtain. The bosses have the funds to manipulate the system and take advantage of the Thai technique of making contact with prominent and rich people to get things done. A powerful contact can out rank someone who is technically higher up the social scale or ostensibly in a top position.

It's not what you know; it's whom you know.

Ensuring witnesses can be brought to court, even with the promise of protection schemes and victim compensation, is never easy. Judicial proceedings often get stopped part way through when one party will agree to accept an out of court compensation settlement. We saw that in the HSBC money laundering case in the United States in December 2012 where the bank was fined $1.8 billion because of proven collusion with Mexico's Sinaloa and Colombia's Norte del Valle cartels.

Money payments can change people's minds about giving witness evidence or bringing charges.

Even in countries where witness protection schemes are strong, this remains a problem. Japan has successfully introduced procedures that allow witnesses to give evidence anonymously and where the defence is not given full witness details. This is not a common legal concept for countries where justice should be done and seen to be done but is a step that Japan has successfully taken. Many countries, including Thailand, are reluctant to do this and stick to the laws of evidence and transparent disclosure. Plea bargaining can sometimes result in compromises and this middle way of avoiding conflict and getting to a resolution is certainly a Thai trait. In the long term, it can have an unhelpful impact on the successful prosecution of mafias.

National security is treated seriously. But it is difficult to achieve in a society that values individual freedoms and a laissez-faire approach (*mai bpen rai*) to solving a difficulty or crisis. The concept of individual freedom is important in this country. The Thais do not regard bureaucracy from on high with much affection.

For them, they want to avoid conflict. They take the attitude: Let things be. It is not our business. It does not affect us. At all costs, loss of face must be considered. The rules of hierarchy cannot be changed that easily and quickly. These are all factors that give organised crime bosses a distinct advantage.

Facts are frequently stranger than fiction. Figures vary on how much of the economy is controlled by Mafiosi. The best estimates are sheer guesses. Many billions of baht per year would not be too fanciful a figure.

In the classic film, *"The Hill,"* a movie about the callous treatment of military prisoners in Libya and starring Sean Connery, the regimental sergeant major is trying to find out who is the guilty party of some flouting of the rules amongst his group of prisoners. There is no positive evidence to suggest who the perpetrator is and no information is forthcoming from the prisoners. On the face of it, no one can therefore be found guilty and punished. Some joker within the ranks rather humourously points out that, without proof of who the guilty soldier is, the RSM has no case. The sergeant major's reply removed any doubt about how such incidents can be dealt with, mafia style.

Line up. I will punish every tenth man.

Maybe this example from fiction is the only realistic model that can be used to counter the secrecy and power of organised crime and its ability to avoid enforcement of the law. An unfair but down-to-earth solution?

Innocent citizens will almost certainly get caught up in any attempts by the government to attack organised crime. As in wartime, civilian populations are not exempt from collateral damage, violence, and death when ruthless action is sanctioned.

The 2003 war on drugs in Thailand reduced drug dealing but, as in other countries, the real movers and shakers behind this trade were invisible players and went unhindered and unpunished. While the purge undoubtedly saved lives, innocents also got killed. There has been political fallout ever since over the motives of the politicians involved in ordering the crackdown. Extra judicial remedies rightly attract criticism from human rights groups. Better and more successful strategies need to be found.

As the history of other countries shows, where there are military dictatorships and weak democracies, extra-judicial solutions are common. Balancing the need for justice and fairness with such pragmatic but illegal actions is constantly the subject of debate. And that balancing act is made more difficult when one has to consider the attitudes and views that are ingrained in individual societies and the influence of the élite.

Thailand has its own unique set of cultural attitudes and ideas.

Conclusion

Piecing together the Thai Jigsaw

Oh, East is East and West is West
And never the twain shall meet

We have reached the end of *Thailand Take Two* and have covered a lot of ground together.

Was Kipling right that the West and the East can, with understanding and the will to do so, be brought together?

Having *"looked each other between the eyes,"* can the *twain* meet?

Or are the cultural differences too great?

Can the *farang* and the Thai work at understanding each other's cultures and points of view?

Thai society is very structured. Hierarchy is a powerful force that cannot easily be questioned and affects the lives of all Thais. They value individual freedoms only when they do not conflict with the strong loyalties and social responsibilities they have with those they live and work with. Few Thais could ever be said to be non-conformist in their attitudes and beliefs.

The political crisis in early 2014 attracted protesters wanting the current Prime Minister to resign because her government was seen as corrupt and too powerful. Their dilemma was reconciling their grievances with the parliamentary opposition's stance on doing away with the ballot box and setting up an unelected "people's council." Many Thais that were able to get around the opposition cordons still felt uneasy in supporting a system taking away their right to vote and putting in place a government formed from the great and the good. They wanted an end to corruption but were fearful of moving away from the established Thai cultural attitudes of the class system. Thais feel there are others more important than themselves. The notions of "one man, one vote" and "all men are equal" are not powerful ideologies for the Thai. The crisis showed that the cultural influences of hierarchy and *mai bhen rai* are still very strong and that it will take some time to construct a form of democracy that will be consistent with what one might call "Thainess."

Thais follow their cultural ground rules as much as they understand and accept, whenever possible, the tolerant Buddhist attitude of *mai bpen rai*. They avoid conflict and confrontation, and keep a smile on their faces, whatever emotions they may feel inside.

They are an enigmatic people, whose worldview is not easy for us to comprehend. In a society with such a wide inequality between the rich and the poor, Thais have to accept the cards that they have been dealt but can be extremely jealous of other people who are better off than they are. They can be envious of a foreigner's perceived wealth and seemingly easy and comfortable way of life.

Some have a need to show off. How they are perceived is important to them, reality is secondary. Appearance over substance.

Their love of *sanuk* (fun) contrasts with a shy and modest nature. Thais are cautious when forming firm friendships but become strong pals or buddies once the ice is broken. That is true of Thais whether those they meet are Thai or *farang*.

Thais can be caring and compassionate while being utterly ruthless and not able to see reason in the way Westerners would understand the meaning of that word. Fervent nationalism and love of their country is coupled with individual greed and the survival of the fittest. There are cases where Thais have been scrupulously honest in returning lost property; and cases where they would instinctively pocket it. Their lifestyle can appear simple and uncomplicated at the same time as it is full of intricacies and complexities that we Westerners can have difficulty in fully understanding. Thais need to follow the unwritten rules and traditions that have governed this amazing land for centuries.

Whether a resident expat or a traveller in Thailand, you will enjoy a better experience during your time here if you get into the Thai way of life. To get to know the Thais and Thailand, you will need to make the first move. Meeting ordinary Thais, rich and poor, outside the main tourist areas and trying a few words of their language will allow you to see things from a different perspective.

The language is not easy to learn or speak, whatever the Thai may say. But it does not matter. Try a few words anyway. *Mai bhen rai*. Above all, smile.

The pitfalls are easy to avoid. Be laid-back and accept some compromise. Do not appear angry or raise your voice. Copy the Thai and speak softly rather than loudly. Never let them get the impression that you are talking down at them because you consider western attitudes, ideas, and experiences are superior. Do not make even seemingly innocuous remarks that could be taken as a criticism of the Thai or his country. He will lose face. You will lose respect.

Thai society is interestingly multifaceted but not easy to understand. *Thailand Take Two* offers a different and sometimes surprising perspective of the country and its people. The stories and scenarios that are illustrated may have given you a very different *take* on life here from what is seen at first glance.

Something you have read in this short introduction to Thais and Thailand may have intrigued or surprised you. It may be at variance with what you previously thought about this country. It may be something you had never thought of before but now see in a new light. Maybe it is something you have already noticed but did not fully understand. Whatever you do, keep an open mind and continue to observe what is going on around you. Every day I see or hear different aspects of their lifestyle. I am sure you will too.

Chook dee na krap. Good luck.

Appendix 1

Thailand's Political Journey

Thailand Take Two illustrates and portrays how Thai and western societies are so dissimilar.

For a complete understanding of Thailand and its people, it is helpful to look at how the country has developed politically and how it continues to change. One needs to remember, though, that historical facts can often be distorted and sources are not always unbiased. There is a shortage of well-documented material that is reliable. Few scholars consistently agree with one another.

It may be useful to refer to parts of this appendix when reading *Thailand Take Two*.

This appendix tries, however difficult the task appeared to be, to give the reader a short concise history from 1238 to the present day. At a little over 6000 words, this does not claim to be a complete narrative of 775 years of Thai politics. Its purpose is to complement the social differences that we have discussed in this book and put them in a historical perspective.

I appreciate that dates and facts are not everyone's cup of tea, but a quick read of at least some of this section may pay dividends in really understanding Thailand. You may see parallels between Thailand past and present.

In **1238** Poo Khun Sri drove the Khmers out of what is now the central part of the kingdom of Siam, (as Thailand was called until 1938), and founded the *Sukhothai* dynasty. For some 130 years, the kings ruled in a paternalistic way under broadly Buddhist concepts. Although Poo Khun Sri is sometimes regarded as the first king of Siam, the country was not in fact ruled by just one monarch.

It was not a united country. Different princes and officials administered different regions, and they held power solely in their own localities. Their armies had exclusive command only in those parts of the country where they held influence. The movement of armies was hampered by Siam's poor road network, which made communication within the country slow and difficult.

Thailand Take Two has given examples showing how essential the social model of a strong family is to a Thai. The Sukhothai royal dynasty governed by believing their strong rule was good for the family and the people. In the same way that parents believe they are doing their best for their children by being strict, protecting them, and ensuring they do as they are told.

The next dynasty was that of *Ayutthaya* which ruled from **the mid fourteenth century until 1767** when the Burmese sacked the city of Ayutthaya. This ruling house similarly did not have power over the whole of Siam. It had a more hierarchical and feudal structure than that of the Sukhothai and could be said to have paved the way for a form of absolute monarchy. The kings believed they had a right to rule.

Although their control was not total, they were successfully able to hold a balance of power between many of the other princes and nobles by playing one faction off against another. Astute diplomacy and tough negotiating kept them in check.

All countries use political intrigue. Playing one interest group off against another is as common in present day Thailand as it was in the past, and mirrored what was happening in Europe and the rest of the world.

The Ayutthaya dynasty began creating a stratified society through which they could manage their subjects. Today, we have a hierarchical system that has distinct levels within which everyone knows his or her place, an ideology inherited from that dynasty.

History shows us the links between these two periods of just over 500 years and the present day Thailand we see in *Thailand Take Two*.

It was King Taksin who repelled the Burmese from Ayutthaya in **1767** and established his royal court in Thonburi on the outskirts of Bangkok. His reign lasted just fifteen years; he had become ill and sought refuge as a monk in a monastery. His top general, Tong Duang, took over and crowned himself Rama I, establishing the Chakri dynasty in Bangkok in **1782**.

Rama II was on the throne from **1809 to 1824**. The period was known as the golden age of literature. Apart from a rebellion by King Taksin's son, who was laying claim to the Chakri throne, the reign was peaceful. Rama II's son, who went on to become the king's minister of trade and foreign affairs, quickly put down the revolt.

Rama III ruled from **1824 to 1851** and made the first tentative steps towards making Siam a nation state. The people were becoming more united and had a sense of solidarity in being Thai. Trade was fostered, particularly with China, and commerce within Siam became more business like.

Today, we see how nationalistic and proud of their country the Thais are. Their egoistic self-confidence and inward-looking thinking, traits that we have already seen, stem from this period.

Under Rama IV, King Mongkut (**1851 – 1868**), monopoly income earned by businesses owned by the Crown was slowly replaced by revenue from commissions and taxes on trade carried out by Thai and foreign businesses. The country was opening up to the world. In **1855,** the Bowring Treaty was signed between Siam and Britain allowing free trade subject to a 3% import duty. Agreements with other European countries, America, and Japan swiftly followed. Free trade meant that families other than the king's were taking good profits from the increasing world trade.

The hierarchical system under the Ayutthaya kings was changing towards a class system based on wealth and trade. The king still ruled as an absolute monarch in an increasingly united Siam and was very much in control of his kingdom, but business hierarchies were developing. Elites were being formed which would be powerful but which still owed their existence to the monarch. Big business, the military, prominent land-owners, the "great and the good", all operate within Thailand's constitutional monarchy, co-existing alongside the democratically elected government.

King Mongkhut's prudent strategy of granting trade treaties with other countries resulted in avoiding the territorial invasion by foreign armies and the imperialism that was imposed elsewhere in the Far East. Partly because of the king's foresight and diplomatic skills, Siam has never technically been colonised. *Thailand Take Two* gives illustrations where the Thai people's mindset would, in any case, be very anti-colonisation.

The Meiji restoration in Japan, at around the same time, similarly countered the trend of colonialism. It set up a capitalist type nation state that ushered in industrial change and economic progress at a faster pace than proved possible in Siam.

Although King Mongkut had effectively broken the threat of colonialism and encouraged Siam to move towards a global trade system, the liberalisation of commerce had an adverse effect on the royal finances. The *Bunnags*, the noble class that was profiting from these newly found trade opportunities, were putting more money into their own pockets than was going to the crown exchequer.

Even today, the present day élite in Thailand is at times indirectly criticised for supporting an economic structure that promotes a wide gap between rich and poor.

King Chulalongkorn, Rama V, (**1868 – 1910**), made enormous progress in developing the railway system and improving communications within the country. He significantly modernised the education system and established a regular standing army throughout the realm. Prior to 1887, there was no integrated defence organisation. Interestingly, there were no military coups during his reign.

The King set about reducing the power of the *Bunnags* by replacing their local bureaucratic officials with his own salaried appointees. Under the old feudal *Sakdina* structure of the *Sukhothai* and *Ayuthaya* periods, those appointed to collect money from the local people, the *prai* (serfs), did so in a way that enriched their own families. That was now no longer the case.

Total corruption probably did not stop under the new arrangement but the royal finances improved. While keeping the hierarchical distance between himself, the nobles, and the people, Rama V did away with the practice of his subjects prostrating themselves before him.

He abolished corvée labour and slavery. He wanted a fairer and more modern style of worker relationships. A worker under the corvée structure was obliged to labour; sometimes paid, sometimes unpaid, for a nominated person for life. Many of the slaves were from the debtor prisons, sent there by the courts to work off their debts. The number of slaves released had in any case been diminished since one habitual source of slaves, prisoners taken as spoils of war, had dried up as Thailand moved towards more peaceful times.

The abolition took away much of the power that the landowners had over the people who were beginning to see that their loyalty was more to the king than to the local élite. The monarchy was strengthened as a result. Power and control was moving away from this upper class landed gentry but there were no checks and balances on the monarchy. Historically the land ownership class was based in Bangkok. It was only one hundred years later that a property owning middle class appeared in the outside provinces. Despite that, most large tracts of land are still owned by Bangkokians.

Salaried officials were consolidated into ministries of the crown, an up-to-date army was established, and Siam became more like the single country that it is today. A nation state that was well on the way to being accepted as a sovereign power.

It was Rama VI (**1910 - 1925**), King Vajiravudh, who accelerated the process that eventually gave Siam one national identity. It was he that stressed the tripartite nature of Siam: Monarchy, Nation, and Buddhism. *Thailand Take Two* repeatedly demonstrates how these three attributes are central to modern day Thai thinking.

Rama VI, and undeniably his father before him, appreciated the better aspects of western thinking, technology, and ideas. Absolute monarchy was promoted as an indispensable part of the strategy of continuing the country's unification. The various ethnic and regional groups started to come together during his reign. Increasing involvement with the rest of the world needed a strong institution to stop any resistance from the élite who may have had interests that were self-serving and not in Siam's best interests. At the time, monarchy was looked on as that institution. If you talk to Thais today, you will hear the same reverence for a benevolent monarchy and a distrust of élitism, even though theoretically Thailand is a constitutional monarchy with a government elected by popular vote.

The Wild Tiger Corps, *Kong Seuh Pa*, founded by the king at his coronation as his ceremonial guard, became a paramilitary group numbering some 4000 men. It was unpopular and disliked by both the civil service and the upper class who saw it as a further brake on their influence in Siamese politics. Some members of the corps were given senior positions in the national army and in **1912**, a group of young army officers made an attempted coup against the monarchy. It failed when one of the officers gave detailed information on the plot to the king's staff.

Later the corps was disbanded as it was seen as conflicting with the concept of having one state army controlled by the Crown. The military was thus consolidating its strength as an important power in the kingdom.

There were coups in 1911, 1912, and 1917.

Rama VII, (**1925 – 1935**), reaped the benefits that Siam was getting from the western world but began to face discontent from within the kingdom. Seeds that had been germinated during the time of the *Kong Seuh Pa* were growing. The middle classes, seeing the greater involvement in political affairs that existed in other countries, were impatient for change.

All would be fine if a compassionate monarch or government acted in the interests of the country, but what if the men in authority were not "good men." This is a theme that occurs later in the nation's politics; and, indeed, was put forward as an idea by the faction called *Pitak Siam* during Prime Minister Yingluck's government in 2012. Who decides who is fit to govern and who is not? Who are the "good men?"

Whether you regard a politician as honest or dishonest, whether you consider he is moral or immoral, is perhaps not that pertinent. If the authorities actually decide who are the "good men" then the decision is made for you. Democracy by and for the people, the electorate, becomes irrelevant.

Rama VII, King Prajadhipok, wrote in 1926 of the monarch: *In the reign that has just ended the King has become a person liable to be influenced by anybody who could gain the ears of a favourite. Every official is more or less suspected of embezzlement or nepotism. What was regrettable was that the court was heartily detested and in the later years on the verge of being ridiculed.*

His reign coincided with the economic crisis that followed the great depression and its repercussions on the national economy, factors that added to the restlessness and desire for democracy emanating from the *Kana Rasadorn,* a group of military officers and civil servants.

Rama VII contemplated a supreme council, *similar to that which existed in Russia*, and began transferring some limited powers to the élite. He advocated that *we should prepare the ground for constitutional monarchy as fast as possible and provide an education appropriate to it.*

His suggestions for organising forms of local administration that might lead to a more democratic government appeared indecisive and failed to materialise. However, they did become a basis for change. The king graciously granted that henceforth absolutism would give way to a monarchy corresponding largely with his own views. Siam became a constitutional monarchy on **28 June 1932**.

Bhutan, by contrast, was still an absolute monarchy in 2006, when their crown prince Jigme took over following his father's abdication. As a younger man, popular with his people, as indeed his father had been, his key rôle was overseeing progress to a democratic constitutional monarchy.

In the UK, America, and elsewhere, politics is influenced by big business. Banks and oil companies seem to pull strings. Countries and governments operate via networks. This is modern capitalism as it is seen everywhere in today's world.

Elected governments do not administer or have power in isolation. Politics works through the creation of powerful lobbies and influential networks. Dr McCargo has commented that for part of its history, (1973-2001), Thailand was centred on the monarchy, working with the elected government and other institutions. Dr Paul Chambers has prepared detailed analyses of the influences that the military has had, at various times, on how Thailand is governed, drawing attention to the highs and lows of their power. Other commentators have shown that networks have, at various times, included the Privy Council, some political parties, big business, moneyed families, media barons, and state agencies.

To a very limited extent, this included the Buddhist *Sangha*, the Buddhist church. Their religious teachings are respected and sometimes taken into account.

Networks can operate both directly and indirectly. In full view or behind the scenes. This short account will not elaborate further as there are many texts that the reader can study independently.

Military men, principally Phahol and Songsuradej, led Siam's first constitutional government and they created a National Assembly in **December 1932**. It was half appointed and half indirectly elected. The people were told that they would be given voting rights once half the general population had attained a primary school education. It was envisaged that this would be in the 1940s.

The administration was essentially a coalition of four distinct groups. The conservative civilian faction led by Manopakorn, who became the first prime minister of the National Assembly; a senior and powerful military group headed by Phahol; a more junior group of army and navy officers led by Phibun; and a younger civilian bloc established by Pridi.

The younger Pridi was responsible for developing an economic plan to deal with the effects of the Depression. He advocated nationalising large portions of land and property that had been acquired over the years by the upper classes. His intention was to increase efficiency in the agricultural and industrial sectors, and improve higher education.

The plans looked too much like a move to communism for the old guard. They were suspicious that his plans for the education sector were motivated by an attempt to bring in fresh people, less influenced by the élite landowning class.

Manopakorn served for six months as PM before Phahol succeeded in taking over the premiership following a coup led by himself and Phibun, a coup that was without doubt aimed at stopping Pridi in his tracks.

In **1933** Prince Bovoradej, a grandson of Rama IV, led a coup against the government and accused them of failing to develop King Rama VII's ideals of constitutional monarchy. The King however was not supportive of further clashes between rival factions in the government and the coup failed. Avoiding quarrels and disagreements rather than dealing with a problem hands on is a trait that you will note throughout Thai history.

While abroad for medical treatment, Rama VII engaged in lengthy communications with his government, making it clear that he was concerned at the undemocratic and autocratic path that the regime was following, and the lack of individual freedoms. On **2 March 1935,** he abdicated, saying that: *I am willing to surrender the powers I formerly exercised to the people as a whole but I am not willing to turn them over to any individual or any group to use in an autocratic manner without heeding the voice of the people.*

Prince Ananda (Rama VIII) thus became king at the age of nine and ruled until his sudden death in June 1946 at the age of 20. For much of his reign he was abroad pursuing his education and the government (effectively a regency with few checks and balances to control it) continued its programme.

Siam came out of the gold standard, spending on education and the military were increased, local and provincial governments were set up, and elections were held for the first time in **November 1937.**

In **December 1938,** Phibun became prime minister. Phahol, Phibun, and Pridi had achieved much in five years. Phibun was the strong military man; Pridi was the liberal idealist. Once settled in the seat of prime minister, Phibun became more right wing and dictatorial. A known admirer of Mussolini, he also held anti-Chinese views. Taxes were imposed on Chinese businesses and many Chinese schools had to close down.

Political opponents suffered the same strong-arm tactics; many were punished or exiled. Media censorship was prominent and pro-Axis propaganda encouraged. The government's powers of arrest were strengthened. There were more portraits of Phibun on the streets than that of the King. It was at this time that the country's name changed from Siam to Thailand, reinforcing the point that the nation was for the Tai races (Thai, Lao, and Shan.)

You can't take Thailand out of the Thai.

Nationalism and pride in one's country was a continuing theme under Phibun. National holidays replaced the traditional royalist dates. The Chinese got no mention.

In today's Thailand, the Thai-Chinese, third or fourth generation immigrants, are prominent in the country's business community and in government. The military are still a major force within Thailand's networks of power.

In **June 1940,** Phibun signed a treaty with Japan hoping it would assist in reclaiming, from Laos and Cambodia, the territories that France had taken from Siam in 1893 and 1904. There was collaboration with Japan when Thailand attacked South Vietnam in **January 1941.** Both Britain and the United States came down strongly against Thailand, fearing further Thai territorial expansion.

Until Japan intervened and forced the French to relinquish their claim to the disputed territories, Vichy France and Thailand were constantly in dispute.

On **8 December 1941,** Japan, sending forces into Thailand from the South and from Cambodia, occupied the country. After some brief resistance to this attack, Phibun choose to surrender and formed an alliance with the invader, who was allowed to move its troops through the country to attack Burma and Malaya.

Japan turned a blind eye when Thailand annexed the Shan and Kayah states in northern Burma and parts of northern Malaya. Thailand declared war on Britain and the United States in **January 1942.** The Thai ambassador in Washington received the declaration but he did not officially convey it to the US government. In a sense, they had it both ways. They had declared war but could be said not to have done so. What Welty has referred to as "doing but not doing at the same time." An often-used Thai tactic of navigating troubled waters. Using cleverly thought-out strategies and being pragmatic is typical of the Thai.

Bending like the bamboo in the storm, giving a little in the short term in order to reap greater long-term benefits.

Pridi, technically the regent in the King's absence, led the resistance movement within Thailand, setting up training camps and establishing airfields where British and American airplanes could bring in supplies. Initially it had limited impact.

The Thai economy was suffering through not being able to export rice to its usual markets, and the allies were heavily bombarding Bangkok.

In **1944,** Phibun was removed in a coup. The National Assembly reconvened and the liberal politician, Khuang, became prime minister. Covering all bets, he returned the British territories that Phibun had annexed while taking care not to annoy the Japanese who were still on Thai soil.

On **15 August 1945,** the Japanese forces surrendered and the Thais formally changed sides. America refused to sanction full war reparations claimed by Britain and other nations for Phibun's support of the Japanese and his complicity in the atrocities on the Thai sections of the infamous Death Railway.

The military was now weakened. The government became increasingly unpopular for having chosen the losing side in the war.

In **1946,** Pridi's civilian party won the general election, the first in which political parties were allowed to canvass, and he became prime minister just after King Rama VIII's return from Europe in December 1945. The King had been away for the best part of 10 years during the government of Phibun and the war years. Following the King's sudden death in July 1946, his younger brother King Bhumibol succeeded to the throne.

In early **1947,** Pridi agreed to hand back some further French territory in exchange for a promise of American aid and support in joining the United Nations. Pridi was forced to resign in **August 1947** and a military controlled government was formed. In **April 1948,** the army re-installed the exiled Phibun as PM and Pridi left Thailand for China, never to return to his native land.

Phibun's second term as premier lasted over 9 years. During this time, the cold war was taking hold and North Vietnam increasingly showed up as a communist threat. America was keen to support the Thai government in its own fight against communism.

Political opponents and some members of the wartime Free Thai underground were arrested. Counter coups by Pridi supporters in **1948, 1949**, and **1951** all failed. The army was back in power.

A senate was created by the 1949 constitution but Phibun reverted to the 1932 version in **1951**, in effect reducing the National Assembly to a non-elected body. Economically, Thailand was booming through increased rice exports and further American aid.

The military, particularly some of Phibun's rivals in the army, appeared to be getting disillusioned with their leader and a bloodless coup took place on **17 September 1957**. Thanom became PM though the power really lay with Field Marshall Sarit, who became premier in **1958**. Sarit held the position until his death in **1963** when Thanom assumed office for a second time.

Sarit and Thanom were not western educated or influenced; they were dedicated monarchists who had strong beliefs about the Thai class and hierarchy systems. They saw a need to make the monarchy more prominent. Fervently anti communist, they saw military control in government as Thailand's best defence against that political danger. America's involvement in Vietnam undoubtedly meant that Sarit could count on full support for his dictatorship from his American allies.

The chosen destination for American soldiers on leave from duties in Vietnam was Thailand. The country gained financially from the increased revenue that rest and recuperation (R. & R.) brought. The *mia chao*, women traditionally hired by the month by rich Thais, now found a new and lucrative market amongst soldiers on leave from the Vietnam war zones.

It also gave Thais access to a western culture previously available only to the rich cliques who could afford to travel abroad and mix with Westerners. The ordinary Thai's life was changing. A middle class was now tentatively beginning to have some influence.

Dissatisfaction was not entirely absent. During Rama V's reign, local landowners had been allowed to take large expanses of land for themselves. What became apparent many decades later was that this resulted in almost a third of the population not owning any land. Improved standards of education in the schools and universities resulted in some younger Thais questioning the present state of affairs. Businesses too wanted change. Student protests concentrated on land loss, high rents, oppressive policing, corruption in the establishment, poor infrastructure, and the core poverty of the majority.

Although Thanom was initially able to hold on to power, he orchestrated a coup in **1971** in an attempt to strengthen his position, establishing himself as military dictator. There was open conflict. Despite the continued ban on political gatherings, unrest grew between June and October 1973, culminating in the riots of **14 October 1973**. Police were using teargas and there was gunfire. The military were summoned and tanks were soon on the streets.

King Bhumibol condemned the government and sent Thanom and his two principal co-conspirators, Praphas and Narong, into exile. He appointed Dr Sanya, a respected law professor, as the new prime minister. These events had popular support and showed that the monarch could act as a hands-on ruler as well as fulfilling the official three-fold function of advising, encouraging, and warning the government.

By **1975**, the monarchy in Laos had fallen and communism in Cambodia and Vietnam had taken deep roots. Thais were beginning to join the party, mainly in the rural areas, but there were also middle class splinter groups in the major towns. Fears of a political regime, similar to that of their neighbours, taking hold in Thailand were getting stronger. Excuses were often found for opponents of the government; in the universities, media, and civil service, to be rounded up or dealt with extra judicially. Paramilitary organisations such as the right wing Village Scouts and Red Gaurs were said to be involved.

When Thanom was invited to return and enter a royal monastery, tension was again inflamed. Anti communist witch-hunts, real or imaginary, became frightening experiences.

On **6 October 1976,** the state of affairs deteriorated and there was a massacre at Thammasat University in Bangkok. A future prime minister, the right wing Samak, was alleged to have been implicated in much of the violence and paramilitaries were brought in. Some 46 students were reported killed while many fled abroad or up-country. Later that evening the military were drawn in and took over the government, installing Thanin, a judge from the hard right of politics, as PM. Regarded only as a strongman, he was inept at controlling the economy and investors, including those from overseas, were losing confidence.

Inevitably, a further coup took place in **October 1977** and General Kriangsak became premier and offered an amnesty to the communists. In **1979,** China decided to stop supporting Thai communists in return for Thailand taking in Khmer Rouge forces fleeing after the invasion of Cambodia. Knowledge of Khmer's human rights crimes made some Thais think twice about their former communist sympathies. The Chinese diplomatic initiative thus had the result of sounding a death knell for Thai communism.

Kriangsak was removed in **1980** and the army commander in chief General Prem, a future Privy Council president, took charge and remained in office for over 8 years.

In **April 1981,** the "Young Turks," a group of young army officers, took over the National Assembly to try to force social change. The attempt was quickly rebuffed and an amnesty given. Towards the end of **1982,** many communist fighters were persuaded to lay down their arms, ending any significant support that still existed for the party in Thailand.

The **April 1983** elections overwhelmingly returned Prem to power, now as an elected politician rather than as an appointee. His popularity won him successive elections in 1983 and 1986 but it was time for new blood and in **1988,** General Chatichai took over the reins. For less than three years. In **February 1991** a clique of generals from the Royal Military Academy, led by Sunthorn and Suchinda, accused Chatichai of allowing certain parts of the military to make corrupt profits from government contracts. In the name of the National Peace Keeping Council, they placed Anand in Chatichai's place, though they ensured they were in control.

Suchinda, one of the coup leaders, won the **March 1992** elections, so there was little hope that a non-army government was really being formed. Demonstrations led by a former Bangkok governor, Chamlong, led to a dispute with Suchinda's forces and hundreds died. King Bhumibol called Suchinda and Chamlong to the palace and told them to find a peaceful solution.

The monarch's famous intervention, with the two generals kneeling low before their King, was televised live to the nation. There was popular support for the King's involvement.

This was an example of a mediation of last resort. Some Thais have called this a form of royal democracy. It is better described as being consistent with the generally accepted view that a monarch's duty is to step in when parties cannot agree or a government fails. Most, if not all, Thais would support this analysis in principle.

Their feelings for King Bhumibol as their monarch are so strong. His contribution may not have been in accordance with any written constitution, but a monarch, because he is not directly involved in day-to-day politics, can act in the best interests of his kingdom when the need arises.

Suchinda resigned and Anand was re-appointed. There were no further coups until 19 September 2006, when the perceived view that there would be no further interference by the military proved wrong.

The **September 1992** elections brought in a Democrat party Prime Minister, Chuan, whose term in office lasted until 1995. A coalition under Banham was formed in **1995** but, with many rumours of corruption, his government fell in **1996** and Chavalit became premier. In less than one year, he too lost office. His handling of the **1997** Asian financial crisis and the baht's devaluation had sealed his fate. The civilian Chuan came back to office and undertook successful negotiations with the International Monetary Fund.

Four years later, in the run up to the **2001** elections, Thaksin's Thai Rak Thai party called for a change of tactics. The party's name means, "Thais love Thais," positively reflecting the Thais' patriotic love of their country but, more regrettably, their negative xenophobic tendencies.

Thaksin was unhappy about so much power being yielded to the IMF and campaigned against corruption, organised crime, and the drugs trade. All were popular measures and he won by a wide margin of 40%, the highest ever recorded. He was the only Thai premier ever to finish a full term in office and in fact went on to win a second time in 2005.

In **2002,** Thaksin replaced the Southern Border Provinces Authority, set up by Prem in the 1980s, with squads from the regular police. Far from relieving tensions, the result was a series of extrajudicial killings, 850 were reported in the period **January 2004**

to mid 2005. The King stepped in and asked for the police and army to cooperate and stop the bloodshed. Possibly reluctantly, Thaksin set up the National Reconciliation Commission.

Criticism of Thaksin remained. His opponents detested his attempts at controlling the media, his business relationships with the Myanmar generals, his rôle in the extrajudicial killings during the war on drugs, and possible corruption during the bids for Bangkok's new airport and other business deals.

The media mogul Sonthi started attacking Thaksin on his news programmes. The prime minister retaliated by removing them from the airwaves. Sonthi and his People's Alliance for Democracy party (PAD or yellow shirts) claimed that Thaksin's sale of the family company without paying capital gains tax was immoral.

Although both the Thai Stock Exchange and the Revenue department accepted the transaction as perfectly legal, the controversy did not go away and mass protests were regularly held. Thaksin called for a vote of confidence from the people and an election was scheduled for October 2006.

On **19 September 2006,** a coup was launched while Thaksin was at the UN, parliament was dissolved, and General Surayud took control until elections could be called in **December 2007**.

Samak won those elections, though without an absolute majority, and governed in a coalition supported by pro-Thaksin parties.

In August **2008** PAD protesters occupied Government House. Samak declared a state of emergency but appeared powerless to get the country back to normal. The Constitutional Court made him stand down as premier in September 2008 because he had hosted a cooking show, a conflict of interest with his rôle as prime minister.

Thaksin's brother-in-law, Somchai, became premier in September. In November, protesters invaded Bangkok's main airport and attempted to intercept Somchai's incoming flight. It was diverted and the premier eventually took refuge in Chiangmai, a northern stronghold of his PPP party, and he governed temporarily from there.

The police could not manage the disorder at Bangkok airport and it was later closed. The military proposed that the PAD protesters should withdraw and the Somchai government resign. Neither side could accept that as a solution. Explosions at the airport continued but the PAD would not allow the police or any other government agency to investigate. In December, the PPP was dissolved for election fraud.

The Democrat party contender Abhisit, with support from a previously pro-Thaksin splinter group, became head of a coalition government in **December 2008**. Anti-Abhisit protests became intense throughout the whole of **April 2009,** an Asean summit was disrupted, press censorship was introduced, and the prime minister declared a state of emergency. The army was called in. The formal siege of Government House ended on 14 April; and the state of emergency, but not the censorship decrees, was withdrawn.

In May 2009, PAD founded the New Politics Party to oppose what it saw as an anti-monarchy faction in the country. The party was fanatically anti-Thaksin and anti-corruption. Its political opponent was the National United Front of Democracy Against Dictatorship, formed by pro-Thaksin supporters still claiming that the 2006 coup was an attempt to displace an elected government with members of what became known as the *Amatyathipatai*, (Elites or Nobles Regime). It contended that Abhisit was not being even handed in his dealings with yellow shirt and red shirt protesters.

In February 2010 $46 billion of assets were seized from Thaksin businesses and clashes opened up again on the streets. In May, Abhisit announced elections for the coming November and it seemed the protests would be called off. However, when it was revealed that only the government leaders would be given an amnesty for their alleged involvement in the riots, the opposition party continued their demonstrations.

The **August 2011** elections saw Yingluck Shiniwatra become Thailand's first female prime minister. She was the younger sister of former premier Thaksin and her government followed principles close to those of the Thai Rak Thai party, (February 2001 – September 2006)

The 2011 election was only the second in the country's history where a party achieved a parliamentary majority. Yingluck campaigned for poverty reduction and national reconciliation, and appeared to be using networks within Thailand's political structure to achieve her goals and remain in power.

In **November 2012**, a group called *Pitak Siam* organised an anti-government rally in Bangkok aiming to overthrow Yingluck's administration and replacing it with a five-year "freeze" on political development. The aim was for elected governments to be temporarily superseded by rule by "good men."

The demonstration lasted only one day and was called off by its leader, a retired army general named Boonlert, when only around 20,000 people came in support. Yingluck had declared a state of emergency in three areas of Bangkok and instructed the police to keep order. The military was not involved. Boonlert resigned as the head of *Patik Siam*, saying he would have no hand in future protests. He said, *the armed forces stood by and did nothing.*

Patik Siam's failure to effect regime change can be contrasted with the successful measures that President Morsi of Egypt took, coincidentally at the same time as Boonlert, to give himself dictatorial powers. That success for the Arab Spring was of course reversed when he was deposed by the military just a few days after the first anniversary of his taking office.

In December 2013, Yingluck decided to dissolve parliament and call fresh elections following the resignation of many MPs on the opposition benches and violent demonstrations by anti-government protesters. She had lasted one year and three months, and under the constitution remained PM until the February 2014 elections when she stood again.

Suthep, an ex deputy to former prime minister Abhisit, led the demonstrations in Bangkok. The protests were initially in opposition to an Amnesty Bill which would have wiped the slate clean, in a spirit of reconciliation, of all pending or completed prosecutions against politicians and activists of both parties. Even when the bill was voted out, the protests continued with Suthep and others demanding an end to elections and the appointment of "good men." It was very reminiscent of the days of Pitak Siam.

This journey through 775 years of Thai history has recorded in brief the events that have shaped and influenced this country. Many sources can be researched for a fuller understanding of this period. It is important to read widely because there is much controversy on the historical accuracy of some of the events discussed. This short piece of some 6000 words does not attempt to list those differing opinions.

The early years of the *Sukhothai* were paternalistic and benevolent, qualities that our illustrations in *Family and Community* show are always endearing to the Thai. The *Ayuttaya* kings established a strict hierarchy that made everyone's position in society clear. Examples of this theme are repeated in many different ways in *The Thai Hierarchy*.

Our potted history is as full of intrigue and deviousness as the stories we have read in *All Thais Cheat* and elsewhere in *Thailand Take Two*. The practical and pragmatic reactions of the Thai to colonisation, communism, and the events of the Second World War are mirrored in several chapters.

About the Author

"Stop. Put on hold the stories you have read or heard about this country. Let's have a fresh look, A Second Take, at the reality that is Thailand"

Matt Owens Rees

Are you sometimes surprised when visiting a foreign country? Do you like discovering a side of people's lives that tourists rarely see?

Matt Owens Rees has written extensively on Thais and Thailand.

Thailand Take Two describes the main characteristics and differences between Thais and Westerners. *A Thailand Diary* is a lighter read with more than 100 diary entries. You can take a virtual look inside the everyday lives and experiences of the Thai people, and how they and foreigners interact in this amazing country.

Through field research and discussions with Thais, either in normal conversation or in the lecture theatre, Matt Owens Rees presents a rich picture of the real Thailand: warts and all. His method is to encourage dialogue but to do more listening than talking.

Despite not being similar in style, his books reflect on some of the observations in "Mai pen Rai Means Never Mind." In his opinion, the best book written on Thais and Thailand. Penned by Carol Hollinger in 1965, its insights are still very revealing and up to date. Sadly, Hollinger passed away at 45 years old before she could see her best selling book in print.

Thailand Take Two and *A Thailand Diary* are dedicated to her.

Escape to Thailand is an account of an expat's experiences and sometimes unease after moving to Thailand. We become "flies on the wall' during his early days and months here, and the reader is invited to reflect on how he or she would have coped in similar circumstances.

The Thai Way of Meekness is a short volume that the author was asked to write to put in layman's terms a doctoral thesis about the early Christian missionaries in Thailand. It is available separately but is included as a free chapter in the author's other titles.

You can follow Matt Owens Rees at mattowensrees.wordpress.com, his twitter address is @mattowens355, and you can email him at brigydon@gmail.com

His Chiangmai, Thailand Facebook page is Matt Owens Rees.

The Thai Way of Meekness

INTRODUCTION

The Thai academic Ubolwan Mejudhon submitted her dissertation, "*The Way of Meekness: Being Christian and Thai in the Thai Way*" and was awarded her doctorate in 1997. It remains a model and thorough examination of the problems Christian missionaries faced when trying to spread the teachings of Christianity in Thailand.

Despite its long title – not untypical given university guidelines on thesis submission – it is a well-researched work. The list of references cited is itself ten pages long.

The Thai Way of Meekness is a commentary on her thesis and attempts to put some of the necessarily academic jargon into layman's language.

What is significant about Ubolwan's writing is that it reinforces and confirms the importance of understanding that Thailand's culture is not the same as that of the West. Her purpose was to analyse, highlight those differences, and show that the failure of the early Christian missionaries in Thailand was due to their lack of that cultural awareness. These were lessons that the early missionaries failed to grasp to any degree. Dr Bradley, (1804-1873), one of the most notable of the early preachers, made just one convert.

Although Ubolwan had to write in an academic style, she does include some personal experiences. Her references to Carol Hollinger's classic, "*Mai Pen Rai Means Never Mind*," are an excellent introduction to the differences between the Thai and western ways of life and liven and strengthen her main arguments.

Thailand Take Two, A Thailand Diary, and *Escape to Thailand* can be read alongside *The Thai Way of Meekness* because all four books look at Thai lifestyles and how they are so dissimilar from our own. All four come to the same conclusion: that Thailand is a fascinating country in which to travel and live if the distinctive mind-sets of the Thai and the *farang* (white foreigner) are understood.

Ubolwan examines the difficulties and frustrations that Buddhist Thais experience while learning about Christianity from missionaries.

Her thesis is that there are several factors that must be addressed by anyone trying to teach or influence people of another culture. In short, understand the society in which you find yourself and integrate into that way of life. Her writing is, therefore, useful for both the missionary and the Westerner living in or visiting Thailand.

She identifies a number of what she calls Thai characteristics. They are in fact very similar to our own list of the concepts and attitudes that influence the character, thought processes, and way of life of the Thai. She is using different words because she is writing academically and in a different context but she describes precisely the same factors that we have identified in our own books. The ideas of no conflict, face, family, the strict class structure, *mai bpen rai*, etc.

Her excellent dissertation is worthy of study in its own right by anyone wanting an in-depth examination of how Christianity has and should be taught in Thailand. She builds up her arguments from a number of different angles and perspectives. It is recommended and well worth reading.

We will not attempt to discuss all her views in detail here. The dissertation is just over 400 pages! Nevertheless, we will make comments and observations on the points she raises while drawing comparisons with the topics that we develop in the various chapters of *Thailand Take Two*.

"*The Way of Meekness: Being Christian and Thai in the Thai Way*" by Ubolwan Mejudhon is archived by The E Stanley Jones School of World Mission and Evangelism, Asbury Theological

Seminary.

THE BASIC THESIS

Dr Ubolwan claims that Thai meekness is an essential part of Thai culture. She talks of power through weakness. She talks of inter-dependence within the family and community.

We have been singing to the same hymn sheet, if you pardon the religious metaphor. While Ubolwan writes of meekness, we write about *mai bpen rai*, the attitude of mind that turns the other cheek and claims that problems and disappointments in life are not always that gloomy and significant. She writes of avoiding conflict and touches on the important subjects of the class system, face, and family values. They are familiar Thai qualities that readers of *Thailand Take Two* and *A Thailand Diary* will already recognise.

When she refers to power through weakness, she is explaining how in the long run the attitudes of no conflict and *mai bpen rai* can win through. And the Thai can "win through" because of the support that comes from family and community in Thailand. It is a sense of camaraderie and belonging with all the potency which that brings.

She says that by being meek, humble, and gentle one can keep self-esteem and still achieve one's goals. Values and pride are kept intact. Their Thai meekness can win through.

She has explained Thai meekness in this way:

"The Thai believe that giving in first for later victory is a sign of inner strength, courage, and wisdom because power comes through weakness."

Thais try to get the best they can for themselves and others in the family and community. They replace arguing with flattery and persuasion while obeying the unwritten rules of hierarchy. They accept compromise and never ruffle people's feathers unnecessarily. They are content with their position in society and readily accept the cards they have been dealt in life. By doing this, they believe they have power over their lives.

Thais seem to acknowledge that some people are better than they are and others are not. Whatever the demerits of that non-western view, it is a stabilising factor in Thai society. Life appears well ordered. In the West, we have rights, entitlements, and there is a notion of fair play and equality. We take for granted the concepts of free speech and democracy. We believe that education and welfare provision should be available to all. A Thai accepts what he gets. He accepts his karma. That must have made the work of converting to Christianity very difficult for the early missionaries.

Westerners tend to rationalise, question, and argue a point. Thais do not do this directly. They prefer compromise and *mai bpen rai* as a solution. And they follow the instincts of their hearts. Ubolwan also suggests that you have to show weakness or vulnerability to be accepted by the Thai. You have to bend a little, she says, to meet them halfway. You have to show that you are prepared to get a feel for their culture and way of doing things. Coming across as being too adamant in your beliefs, not seeing an opposite point of view, will result in your not making much progress in discussions with Thais, whether spreading the gospel or in general conversation.

Being over-assertive when trying to explain Christian doctrine and views may be fine in a western country. It will not succeed in Thailand. Adapt to the culture and go with the flow. Adapting does not mean lowering your western standards. It means you are sensibly making slight changes in order to carry out your task of leading and evangelising. Lessons that are as relevant to all foreigners in Thailand as they are to missionaries.

She uses different words but it is true that you should not assume a superior position with Thais or give any indication that you are right and they are wrong. Use some humility and look for areas of mutual understanding. Never be self-righteous. Thais think that shows a negative colonial type attitude.

She is right when she claims Thais are not naturally assertive. She bases her comparisons on her knowledge of expats and missionaries. Westerners tend to speak directly and a little "in your face." Thais do not. They will at times move away from a problematic situation.

Blessed are the meek, for they will inherit the earth, (Matthew 5.5.), would seem very appropriate to the Thai way of thinking when one considers the weight they attach to *mai bpen rai* and *greng jai* (consideration for other people.)

Ubolwan mentions that Thais refuse to argue when involved in a dialogue or debate. That is an example of the Thai trait of avoiding possible confrontations. She believes there is enormous power in adopting that attitude initially. There will be time later to influence the listener and more convincingly make one's point. Being meek can have its advantages as it encourages deeper thinking and time to reflect. Not easy for the Thais as, while some may have the aspiration for critical thinking, they lack confidence in following it through.

Charm and persuasion comes more naturally to a Thai than arguing and quarrelling. Conversations are never rushed affairs in Thailand.

Speaking calmly without raising your voice is a good lesson to learn. A bit of *sanuk* (the Thai sense of fun and being happy) would not come amiss. Be *jai yen* (cool hearted) and you will achieve constructive dialogue. Never go straight to the point. Practice a bit of sweet-talking first and encourage your hearers to want to listen to you.

Let us look at what she has called the nine Thai Characteristics, the "value clusters" that were researched by Suntaree Komin. She refers to them as orientations. In *Thailand Take Two*, we use fewer technical terms but we cover and describe the same characteristics. Many of them inter-link.

Ego-orientation

Grateful relationship orientation
Smooth interpersonal relationship orientation
Flexible and adjustment orientation
Religio-psychical orientation
Education and competence orientation
Interdependent orientation
Fun and pleasure orientation
Achievement-task orientation

Ego: The Thai has a high level of self-esteem, which is why not losing face is so important in their society. To foreigners, this can give an impression of arrogance, that the Thais think they are always right. If you repeatedly praise a builder in the West, by saying he is skilful and you are impressed with his work, he will think that you are being facetious and "taking the mickey out of him." In Thailand, you will hear the word *geng*, skilful and clever, wherever you go. It is acceptable and almost a required way of engaging with people.

Egoism and a fervent nationalism can indicate a xenophobic outlook. Thais are passionately proud of their nation. They are Thai and no other epithet is required. Calling them God's children, children of the light, sinners, or the saved is not appropriate and should be avoided. Always respect their position on patriotism.

The perceived arrogance does not suggest assertiveness. They do not like being challenged and will not stand their ground in an argument or debate. That is a defence mechanism that Thais regularly adopt to save loss of face. They would rather walk away than question what you are saying.

Be careful how you criticise, particularly in front of their social superiors. Self-identity must never be violated. If it is, it can often lead to physical aggression. Westerners – whether visitors or not – need to be aware that allowing a Thai to lose face or putting them in a situation where they feel they are not getting respect, can have dangerous consequences. The response to the loss of reputation and status is more pronounced here than in the West.

The notion of self is significant and repentance is not for public show. It is private. Self-dependence is valued highly and shows a person has strong character. And although inter-dependence is important there is never an absolute reliance on others. The *greng jai* (consideration towards other people) influence is too strong for that. Ajarn Ubolwan suggests that this can give missionaries a difficult task in convincing the need for acceptance and reliance on God. Difficult but not impossible. One just needs to deliver the message Thai style and with an understanding of the culture.

The lesson for missionaries was not to evangelise using western methods. Do nothing that will result in your convert being belittled. And make sure that you never embarrass or shame. Say nothing that might suggest a conflict of views. Be as indirect as you can when you want to make your case. Use suggestions and hints, and show rather than tell if at all possible. Missionaries should have learned never to talk down to a Thai.

Understand their culture and their different attitude to life. That lesson could be more far-reaching than in just this context of Christian evangelising. We saw that quite clearly in some of the stories described in *Thailand Take Two* and in *A Thailand Diary*.

Grateful relationship: Thais enjoy giving and receiving. This reciprocal giving is called *nam jai* (the Thai notion of giving and sharing.) If you visit a home or family, take a small gift or some food. It is the thought not the value that will count in Thailand.

Even if you are not at home, you may find a small bag of fruit or other food hung on your gatepost. One of your neighbours would have placed it there.

Thais are generally always ready to help others but there can sometimes be reasons when they are a little fearful. At traffic accidents, they may be reluctant to help if there is a possibility that they may be accused in some way. That is understandable and does not detract from their normal helpfulness and eagerness to be a very caring and considerate people. Sometimes Westerners forget that, despite that eagerness to help others, Thais are fundamentally a shy people.

The missionaries should have seen how important family and community are to the Thai, how often they meet and communicate with their neighbours. The different sections of the community live in harmony and support each other. If the workers respect their bosses they will cooperate and help them. The élite, in their turn, take their responsibilities in the community seriously and with a sense of duty.

The dual relationship has mutual benefits and is a stabilising influence within society. The élite consider they are working in the best interests of the populace. The ordinary Thai accepts that that is the natural order of things in their country. Both are "grateful," in Ubolwan's words, for their separate contributions. The evangelists could have capitalised on this by working harder to gain the respect of the Thais. Coming across as if they were colonialists or imperialists – however unintended – and imparting western knowledge in that way, was how their teaching was often received.

Smooth interpersonal: Thais need to feel at ease with one another. This is why they always need to know their place within the Thai hierarchy. And why they are so inquisitive about your age, your job, and your position in society. They must establish where you stand relative to them in the class system before they have any interest in what you say.

Thai Christians who have converted from Buddhism or another religion can be accepted and respected by their communities because the Thai concepts of forgiveness and reconciliation are prominent in Thai culture. Thais like smooth relationships.

The early missionaries might have been better advised to think about bonding and connecting with their potential converts, talking to them on their own level, understanding how Thais interact with one another. They could have accomplished that without losing any of their authority.

The use of *pee* and *nawng*, the Thai words for older and younger in general conversation, demonstrates how crucial an understanding of using culturally accepted language is. Missionaries were often judged on how they spoke. By not using social niceties such as this when they were speaking, they failed to gain the respect of their church members. Using correct and polite language is a prerequisite in this country.

Dressing appropriately and observing proper manners comes naturally to a Thai and is another way of showing one's position to others. Always with a smile and always with some smooth-talk and maybe a little flattery. The early missionaries were always well presented. Dressing down as a token egalitarian measure – western style – had not yet arrived.

In offices, social position and where one is on the power ladder are not determined only by the clothes one wears. Showing status is all-important to the Thai. The size of your desk, or whether you have the key to the private washroom is of crucial significance. For teachers of Christianity, having a high status and honourable reputation in the neighbourhood was what mattered. If they had only understood Thai culture better, they would have obtained that status with very high marks. Their western attitudes let them down.

Not imposing oneself on others, *greng jai*, is a Thai characteristic. Attitudes need to be non-judgmental. Even high court judges will try to resolve cases between the parties if some compromise is possible. Sometimes, as we see in *A Thailand Diary*, even after judgment has been given. They will, as all Thais do, avoid criticism when making a decision. The judge will try to find another way out and encourage or tell the parties to reconcile or compromise. In western courts, judges pass sentences but do not forgive. They leave no room for re-gaining self-respect. Thai thinking is different. It is sensible to weigh carefully what you have to say to a Thai before you talk. Diplomacy, tact, and flattery are virtues.

The police will parade suspects, prior to any court appearance, in front of the TV cameras and the press and will get them to re-enact their alleged crimes. The Thais do not consider this as a humiliation technique. To them it is a stage in repenting and apologising. Western churches do not publicly renounce people. Confessional boxes are private.

Punishment is important in western culture; society confronts and corrects. Thailand looks more towards reconciliation and bonding following a dispute or disagreement. There is of course a tough penal system. But the Thai instinct is in theory one of repentance and forgiveness rather than punishment.

Western democracy strongly believes in the maintenance of law and order as an important part of being governed. Living according to a strict code of morality is a given. Thinking and reasoning is how life is ordered. The brain overrides the heart and emotions. In Thailand, because of the concept of face, regard for feelings and emotions are more paramount.

Corruption and cheating is rife in this country, but the evidence suggests that it is accepted because of the belief that karma will eventually prevail. In the meantime, the other cheek has to be turned to keep relations smooth. Belief in karma is not widely held in the West.

Peer pressure may influence an offender to make amends and this is often achieved indirectly by his appeasing the spirits of his ancestors by apologising and making an offering at the spirit house. In hill tribe areas, spirit doctors may go into a trance and perform a ceremony for the guilty party. Contact with the actual victim and its associated loss of face is avoided. No police involvement or court proceedings are deemed necessary. Harmony is maintained in the community. This animist approach may be followed by the transgressor quietly arranging some compensation to the person he has wronged.

Flexible and adjustment: Trying to find a middle way by seeing life's problems in perspective if they are not that crucial. Not being too rigid or insisting on regulations being obeyed to the letter.

Buddhism stresses the "middle way," finding a compromise. However, Thai Muslims have the same attitudes so it would seem that it is Thainess and not the Buddhist religion that has the stronger influence in society when it comes to their attitude of avoiding quarrels and seeking compromise.

Komin summed it up well. "Principles, rules, policies, and even agreements might not be upheld when weighed against personal relations. Instead, they are dispensable and will be overruled by self and in-group interests." Compromising and taking a more *mai bhen rai* – does it really matter – attitude, seems to be the Thai method. Trying to adjust to the other person's view and trying to be as flexible as one can.

"Self" refers to face; "in-group" refers to family and community.

The missionaries should not have been so serious, formal, and dogmatic with the Thais. They should have appreciated the value that their congregations placed on "face." Showing what you mean by example is more face-saving for the Thai than the normal "telling" or "preaching" technique of most religious teachers. A more casual, indirect, and flexible form of approach should have been found. Talking down to Thais is never a solution.

They needed to fit in with the local families and the community, to be at ease in that environment. An appreciation was needed that interactions, getting along with people within the neighbourhood, was more relevant than the community adhering strictly to rules and regulations imposed from outside. Persuading a Thai is easier if you get him on side first. That is true whether people are being lectured at by the state or by the church.

Whom you know in society can be useful. Cultivating contacts in high places in the community should have been considered. It would have been helpful and, more importantly, the ordinary Thai would have noted their teachers were adopting the Thai way.

Being flexible, accepting compromise, and finding a means of meeting someone half way are Thai attributes that are linked to Ubolwan's smooth interpersonal characteristic.

Thais do not like rigidity or following principles blindly if it detracts too much from their freedom. They will keep to the rules of hierarchy and maintain respect within the family, but they will do that because they are comfortable with it and not because they see them as formal rules that must be obeyed.

Religio-psychical: Most rituals and ceremonies are visual and Thais can relate to them. The negative aspect of this is that it emphasises form and appearance over substance. Being seen in the right attire at a function is more important than the reason why you are there in the first place. It is good to donate to a flood relief project or help in other ways; but one's motivations for doing so should be humanitarian and not for snobbish reasons or showing off.

In a culture where one has to show one's position through one's dress and by emphasising one's contacts and wealth, it is difficult to reconcile the negative attitude of showing off with the necessary mind-set the Thais have in establishing their hierarchical position with others. Attendance at rites and rituals appeals to Thais as they consider it normal to make people aware of their position.

More thought in the planning of church services and meetings and taking advantage of this love of ritual could have increased attendances It is always important to be in tune with your audience or listeners. The missionaries could have paid more attention to bonding techniques and tried to win the hearts and minds of their congregations.

Teaching directly from the bible is too impersonal for the Thai. They accept messengers more readily than the message. The logic of the message is not as important as the integrity of the messenger. Ubolwan emphasises this point when she talks of how missionaries should approach their evangelising in Thailand.

Teaching by example, showing care and consideration to the sick and dying, is better. In religious and non-religious contexts Thais like to understand by seeing, doing and repeating. They learn by rote, story, and parable. The limitation of this is that it does not encourage critical thinking. It is a recurrent problem in Thai education.

Whether or not the idea is understood, Thais have a firm belief in karma. "As you sow, so shall you reap," "What goes round, comes round." But the concept is future oriented. It unfortunately seems to have little bearing on present day-to-day living, morality, and ethics. To the Thai, karma is more relevant for one's future life than for the present day.

Thais sometimes use religion to justify life crises. However, for Westerners this idea of a bad action today having a bad consequence either later in this life or in a rebirth is hard to swallow. Are all illnesses and misfortunes in life attributed to karma from a previous deed? The Christian emphasis is on repentance and forgiveness without any connotation of retribution for previous wrongs.

When some fate befalls a Thai, it is usually put down to that person's karma. Predestination plays a rôle too because many believe that what you do has been preordained. You could not have changed events. You can not always benefit from past karma. Thais look at life and see events unfold in a certain way. They take this as evidence that the theory of cause and effect, which is the basis of karma, must be correct. They observe it as a realistic and true model of how the world operates in everyday life.

Buddhist ceremonies reinforce bonding and integration. They teach generosity and reciprocal giving. They emphasise getting along without altercations, clashes, and arguments. The need for cohesion in the family and the community follows from this teaching. The Christian emphasis is on praying for salvation. This fundamental difference was not always taken into account by those who came to Thailand to convert.

Avoiding disagreements is inbred in the Thai. Dr Ubolwan believes this trait is actually a positive show of meekness. In other contexts, it comes across as not wanting to stand up for what is right and not tackling problems head-on. Is it perhaps an escape mechanism? Trying to shut out the inevitable? Hoping the problem will go away?

Education and competence: Education is largely seen as a way of moving up the hierarchy rather than as a thirst for knowledge. A means to short term benefits with no considerations for the longer-term future. In a sense, no notion of tomorrow. Perhaps the concept of karma replaces it and takes away any need to worry about the future.

Western churches try to educate their flocks. Some of what they teach may strike a nerve because education is seen as a worthwhile endeavour and improves one's knowledge. In Thailand, it is generally seen as a means to earn more money and get a better job. The missionaries might have been better advised to concentrate on their congregations present-day needs and gear their teaching to that end. They could have stressed the "advantages" of Christianity now rather than the importance of salvation in the future.

Educating for the sake of educating does not score highly for Thais. Thais live for today as they accept that they cannot control the future.

Interdependent: Living in a community, working together, getting involved in social events and helping others are instinctive characteristics of the Thai. Reliance on others may also explain why initiative is often not commonly seen. There is no need to solve a problem yourself, if others will be there to help you out.

Many members of staff will go to a funeral and pay their last respects to their boss's mother when she dies. The boss will often attend their weddings and be expected to make a formal speech. If he needs to hit a deadline, however rare deadlines are in Thailand, then his staff will be there to help him.

This reciprocal attitude shows how much people depend on one another and gain from that experience. In small communities, everyone knows everyone else. People know what is going on around them. You will hear loudspeaker systems in most Thai villages and hamlets. The twenty-first century equivalent of "jungle drums." The speaker system is used by the *puyaibaan* (village headman) and by the temples to keep people informed. "Word of mouth" completes the task of ensuring no-one remains uninformed or off message for long. Well-ordered communications breed well-ordered interdependence.

Men such as Bradley could have taken greater advantage of the Thais inclination to talk with others in their communities at every available opportunity. The Thais are great talkers and communicators. A chance to get the locals to spread the gospel for the Church was missed. Interdependence could have been used as a resource to communicate Christian ideas and thoughts.

While most Thais will not display their emotions, they have no such reluctance when it comes to spreading comments and bits of information. Thais do not regard talking about other people as being indiscrete. What may be taken as "gossiping" is actually a form of communication and community bonding.

Rather than directly confronting someone, hints are discreetly dropped by this method of gossiping with your friends. They will pass the message on so that the person you are commenting about is put in the picture. Thais use intermediaries a lot when they want to get something done or have a bone to pick with someone. It is a less assertive way of problem solving and avoids any possible loss of face.

Reprimanding your worshippers, whether for perceived sins or minor transgressions, is not a feature of western religions. Confessions made silently in church or in the privacy of the confessional box is how *farangs* deal with sin. The Thai way of reprimanding is to make subtle comments and to use go-betweens. In this way, they help the transgressor to come to terms with his actions and encourage him to understand within himself what he needs to do to make amends. It is not a western idea or way of thinking at all. The Thai delinquent will remain within that community with no loss of face. Effectively, members of society are doing the reprimanding in their own subtle indirect way.

Ubolwan believes that following what you have been told without question is an unfortunate harmful by-product of the hierarchy rules. She is right of course. Propaganda and one-sided thinking go hand in hand if people are told to believe that ideas must never be challenged or questioned. Those that came to Thailand to make converts to Christianity should have seen the power that they could have had over a people used to obeying and accepting what those in authority demanded. However, they did not marshal that knowledge or take beneficial advantage of it.

People are dependent on one another at all levels of society, both within their own class or group and outside it. Missionaries should have realised how the Thai hierarchy is ordered and then taught their worshippers in a way that conformed to it.

Ideas of respect for one's elders and senior people at local and central level in the country makes for cohesion in the community. Any benefits that that brings is, however, lost if it is always assumed that those with grey hair must always be right. Some critical and radical thinking is sometimes needed if the status quo is to be modified and progress made towards having a structure where higher and fairer living standards can be achieved. But questioning one's elders is inwardly frowned upon.

Adapting to the culture of this country by teaching by means more consistent with it and taking advantage of their position as senior members of the hierarchy, the missionaries could have presented a more successful strategy for their envangelising.

Reconciliation is an idea that is well understood because it emphasises non-conflict. For the Thai, bonding is about family, community, and workplace. For the foreigner living here, it is about integrating. Ubolwan shows that the pressures within Thai society encourage close involvement with family and community. Both the missionary and the expat can gain from this. Those teaching the gospel could have made their sermons and lessons more family-oriented by getting closer to church members and by involving themselves in the community.

Fun and pleasure: Humour helps defuse solemn circumstances. A little flattery and some chitchat makes for smoother social relationships. The Thais use puns a great deal when speaking (though you will rarely find them using sarcasm, not cruel sarcasm anyway). They can tease you in a friendly way.

Thai humour is a dry humour.

A pregnant lady was x-rayed and the results showed that the baby had no head. After many prayers, the baby was born perfectly formed. The x-rays had in fact been totally wrong. The consultant commented that he was glad the praying had not continued for too long. The baby may then have had several heads! A true story.

Thais add *sanuk* (fun) to almost all that they do. They try to make work enjoyable and pleasurable.

I was browsing at a plant stall and a Thai asked the seller for a "farang" (a fruit). I asked him if he wanted to buy me! (farang is also the word Thais use for a white foreigner.)

Londoners use cockney "back chat"; Thais use *kham peuan* or *kham klap*. They find word play funny. That will always get a laugh.

Delicious or tasty in Thai is *aroi dee*. Say, *aree doi* (which is completely meaningless) – swapping the syllables around – and you will have everyone laughing.

Smiling and laughter is commonplace in this country. As we have said, Thais were born with smiles on their faces. It is probably the first indication you will get of the importance the Thai gives to living without conflict and having the smooth relationships to which Ubolwan refers. Smile and the problem may go away.

Westerners were quite surprised to see smiles and dancing and to hear laughter during Nelson Mandela's funeral in December 2013. It makes the point that different cultures see smiling and laughter differently from us. To the South Africans it was a time to celebrate his life and achievements. There was no lack of respect.

A less rigid and less authoritarian approach by those preaching to the Thai members of their churches may have gained more converts. A little humour in the right place. Bringing a little *sanuk* (fun) into the services would have gone down well. Involving the community when they meet in church and encouraging them to talk and discuss amongst themselves in a friendly social gathering can be very helpful. Getting them to narrate some of their own experiences in finding Christianity would have been a good strategy and very acceptable to the Thais. They love discussing how others live and conduct their lives.

Achievement-task: While teamwork and getting on with colleagues is essential (and to the Thai also needs to be fun) task achievement through deadlines and budgets is a tad anathema. You will see few control freaks in Thailand. *Mai bpen rai* is too powerful. To the Thai, ambition does not have great significance. It is not part of their worldview. Their principal economic theory is one of self-sufficiency rather than striving in the global marketplace.

What is crucial is getting on with one's job, with one's life, on a daily basis. Higher ideals of ambition are not that critical. Today matters more than tomorrow. Yes, karma can be a forceful notion. Its benefits and consequences are, however, normally taken as considerations for the after-life and not for today or tomorrow.

Meditation is not future oriented and is a common practice amongst Thais. It concentrates on an absence of thought and physical movement. A stillness of mind and body. There is no concern for the future and, consequently, no feeling of sadness or depression. Such a meditative state is difficult to attain but can be of immense value and benefit by bringing calmness and peacefulness to mind and body. It does not, though, encourage deep and critical thinking.

CONCLUSION

In *Thailand Take Two* and in *A Thailand Diary*, we referred to Thai bashers and Thai apologists amongst the expat population. Those that only see the bad side of the country and those that only ever view Thailand through rose-tinted glasses. Dr Ubolwan's research suggests that that is also her experience. "Most missionaries and Thai Christians have either totally negative or totally positive ideas about Thai culture."

Although I agree with her overall comment on the expats she has met, I would add that she is referring to a minority of the *farang* population, albeit a vociferous one. Most foreigners here get on with their lives quietly and blend in to the very different culture that is of the very essence of Thailand. They do not make the same negative or extreme noises that the bashers and apologists engage in when they hold forth in the bars and on the internet forums.

In her dissertation, Ubolwan comments on the habit of bearing minor grudges and the subtle art of indirectly cold-shouldering someone who is out of favour. Thais never forget an insult and you would need to work very hard indeed to get back on side with them. The missionaries should have chosen a softer and more subtle means of persuading and converting. Anything that smacks of criticism of a Thai or his country will make a bad impression.

Aggressiveness, loudness of speech, and boasting will earn you a snub from Thais. They will smile while delivering it. There are many versions of the Thai smile. It can be used to laugh away sorrow or disappointment as well as to cover embarrassment. It is not always an expression of happiness as Westerners would suppose. The smile covers up a multitude of different emotions.

The Thais, as others from the Far East, have been called inscrutable. Not easy for Westerners to read their minds or understand what they are thinking. They don't wear their hearts on their sleeves. Never assume one can get any clues from their expressions. Think Thai. Trying to learn and understand Thai cultural nuances is not easy but always worth the effort if your goal is to influence or convert.

The early missionaries were possibly too fanatic, too assertive, and confrontational in their attempts to persuade and to teach the lessons of the gospels. They attempted to indoctrinate with what they considered were self-evident truths. There were very few converts in the early days because the pace of attempted conversion was geared to western teaching methods and the pace was too fast.

Better to have sown the seeds of Christianity and allow the Thai to develop his beliefs in his own time. Giving real-life examples of how a Christian conducts himself by following Christian teachings is a steadier approach to conversion than expecting Thais to accept without question what is written in the bible. Although no Thai would dream of challenging a Thai superior, the missionaries should have considered encouraging their flock to engage in some discussion as a means of teaching the message of Christianity.

The phrase "take that as gospel" would be bewildering to a Thai because you are not explaining why he should accept your doctrines. Not giving him reasons and examples to which he can relate in his daily life. Accepting something as an act of faith only comes after conversion. Thais will understand creation and redemption if they are not force fed the concepts and provided the images fit their experiences and there are clear explanations of the theories being taught.

As Dr Ubolwan has said, Thais have strong self-esteem. Attacking this esteem will cause loss of face. Your teachings and views are then harder for them to accept.

Never force a Thai into a corner in a discussion. Thais found the early missionaries, for example Bradley, too strict and rather colonial in their outlook. No understanding of how Thais think or the usefulness of trying to find a middle way. A "we know best" approach that will always fall on deaf ears when talking with a Thai.

Academic theses tend to be very dry affairs but Ubonwan's book lightens up significantly when the author uses examples from her own experience. Quoting formal sources is usually de rigueur in academic texts but her personal comments on how her fiancé was struggling with conversion from Buddhism to Christianity made her realise that you must not rush a Thai.

She had assumed her fiancé had the same high level of faith that she had. He wanted time to find his own way to the truth, to adjust to the new ideas and concepts of a different religion. His friends thought she was being very "un-Thai," in being too forceful and too assuming. That is a sure way to put up unnecessary barriers in trying to get more converts.

She suggested not coming across as *jai rawn* (hot tempered), not being too assertive, and trying to be aware of how a Thai feels. She claimed that a humbler approach to evangelising is more effective. Power through weakness yet again.

She readily accepted that this personal experience taught her much on how Westerners should use a Thai approach to teaching Christianity. Let the Thais be Thais in their own communities. Not only teach in the language that they speak; but also teach in the language of their culture. Not western culture.

Thais respect their parents and teachers. Parents provide love and care and then get life-long respect from their children. Teachers are caring and put in plain words much of the moral and shared "rules" that Thais live by. Both family and teachers have authority in the hierarchy, which is why they gain esteem and are listened to. Ubolwan suggests that the early missionaries could have used that factor to their advantage.

Thais have strong self-will and are not easy to persuade; so gaining respect is essential. Instructing by using parable style examples is more productive than attempts at formal reasoning. Leading by example is effective. Rituals and ceremonies will keep them interested because Thais learn by observing and listening to what their elders and leaders tell them.

It is not a good idea to criticise their superstitions. We have them in the West anyway. Not walking under ladders, not inviting 13 people to a dinner party. A notion that has its origins in the Last Supper where Christ and his twelve disciples were seated around the table and one proved to be a traitor.

The *Loi Kratong* festival symbolises water washing away sin and allowing people to repent. Thais float their *kratongs*, small hand-sized rafts of flowers and candles, on local rivers in a gesture of getting rid of all the ills in their lives. It has great significance to a Thai even if it is grounded in superstition about other gods. The missionaries could have taken the positive aspects of *Loi Kratong*, made comparisons with similar traditions in other religions, and explained the Christian viewpoint on sin, forgiveness, and salvation.

For the Thai, repentance is followed by apologising (by self-volition not force), then forgiveness, then a resumption of bonding. This four-step way of repenting avoids the shaming and ostracising seen in the western model of disciplining and is very different from the more indirect and less rigid approach of the Thai.

Self-will and being disciplined are not good bedfellows. While Thais accept authority (because of the power of hierarchy, family, and community), they have no self-discipline. They will not wear safety helmets on motor cycles because they believe Thais should be "free." They will follow the directions of family and the *puyaibaan* (village headman) rather than a set of laws or regulations. This is their version and understanding of the term freedom. Their definition sometimes sounds as if they are supporting anarchy. The early missionaries would have noticed that characteristic as surely as western teachers do in today's classrooms.

A huge difficulty that missionaries had in convincing a Thai was due to their not appreciating this Thai need to be free to choose.

Winning them over by relating their daily lives to Christian teachings and giving a choice would have been the better plan. Trying to establish a rapport before starting any sort of communication. Progressing slowly and softly gets things done. Ubonwan would suggest "smoothly," "meekly."

Complete insistence on the Christian beliefs that forgiveness and salvation can be achieved only through the mediation of Christ may not necessarily be that essential in the first stages of becoming Christian. Faith and understanding can be built up later. After all, the Dalai Lama commented that not all Buddhists believe in reincarnation at first. That does not stop them being Buddhist.

Don't only thank God for food. Thank the donor also. The Thai will then understand that one is thanking God for getting the donor to donate. It is perceptive of Ubolwan to give this as an example but then she is Thai. Moreover, she is sharing her Thai experiences and heritage to assist evangelising. Her points about thinking in the Thai way are not dissimilar from what we are saying in *Thailand Take Two* and in *A Thailand Diary*. And the message is as relevant to expats and visitors to Thailand as it is to those seeking to spread the word and to gain converts.

For the Thai, religion (whether Buddhist, Christian or any other) is practical and is part of everyday life. They cannot be forced to accept certain views. Religion binds people (family, community) together. As Ubolwan says, "First and foremost, religion is feeling, not reasoning." Thais believe what they see and feel, not what they read. Do good; receive good. Thais understand reconciliation but redemption is a more difficult concept for them. They comprehend relief from suffering but not relief from sin.

Buddhists do not believe in a God as such but they do believe in what the Lord Buddha stands for. Thai Christians think similarly. They accept the underlying concepts as a better way of life but have difficulty in the idea of a supreme being. To them it is not necessary to believe in a God. Tales of fire and brimstone won't impress them.

But explaining how Christianity can be a part of their daily lives can get a message across. They feel the emotions of the crucifixion, for example, but not the concept of a blood sacrifice. That does not lessen their faith.

Ubolwan's main thesis is that one must appreciate the Thai way and the Thai mind if one is to teach Christianity and evangelise successfully. That is a lesson for all of us. Think Thai, integrate, and understand their ways. And that does not mean going completely native.

Her value clusters have strong links to our own model of the pressures and controls that exist in Thai society. Both present a description of some of the interactions of non-conflict, inter-dependence, *mai bpen rai*, hierarchy, face, and family values in Thailand.

Thais can be Christian without losing their "Thainess." They do not have to westernise; we *do* need to appreciate their eastern culture.

Glossary of Thai Words

Used in Thailand Take Two

and A Thailand Diary

There is no single official transliteration system in Thailand for giving a Thai word, written in Thai script, its Romanised English spelling. You will meet several different forms and spellings.

Ajarn; university lecturer
Amatyathipatai; an élite upper-class regime
Amphur; local government office
Angyee; a Thai criminal group
Arai na; what do you want? (abrupt)
Aroi dee; tasty, delicious
Avuso; sinecure, jobs for the boys
Bai see moong; 4pm in the afternoon
Bat prachachorn; Thai ID card
Bhikkhu; the correct word for a Thai monk
Bhikkhuni; a female Thai monk, though without full Sangha rights
Bhusa yong; the blue tape connecting the monks' praying table to the coffin
Bpratet tai; Thailand
Bunkhun; repayment of a kindness received
Bunnag; a 19th century noble class of people

Cao khote; an adviser at family disputes
Chang; builder (also the word for elephant and a brand of beer)
Chao lay; sea gypsy
Chook dee; good luck
Dtrong pai; straight on
Farang; white foreigner
Farangset; French
Farang kit mark mark; the farang thinks too much, too serious
Garuna; formal word for "please," in announcements
Geng; clever, skilful; also a popular nickname
Gnap sop; funeral ceremonies
Goong; shrimp
Greng jai; consideration for people, not wanting to be obligated to others
Jai rawn; hot tempered
Jai yen; cool-hearted, calm
Kana rasadorn; a group of military officers in the late 1920s, early 1930s
Kao niao; sticky rice
Kap, krap, ka; a polite particle at the end of sentences, no real meaning
Kawpkhun krap; thank you (male speaker)
Kawpkhun ka; thank you (female speaker)
Kawp krua gawn; peuan gawn; family first, friends first
Kee niao; mean, stingy, "sticky shit" (don't confuse with kao niao)
Khaek; Muslim, (also the word for guest)
Khom loi; hot air balloon released during Loi Kratong ceremony
Khun; Mr, Mrs, Miss
Khunnang; system of kickbacks, bribes
Kin meuang; the state's percentage cut of a transaction
Kit mark mark; thinks too much, serious
Klong; a canal

Kon asia; an Asian person
Kon lao; person from Laos
Kon mee itthipon; mafia godfather
Kon negro; a Negro
Kon tangchat; foreigner
Kong seuh pa; wild tiger corps
Krapom; yes, agreed (only used by male speakers)
Kratong; hand-sized raft floated during Loi Kratong ceremony
Kroo; teacher
Lamyai; longan tree
Lanna; a northern Thai region (literally a million rice fields)
Lek; small, tiny
Liao kwa; turn right
Longkong; longkong tree
Lung; uncle
Mae ji; A Thai nun (but not a member of the Sangha)
Mae sue; a go-between in marriage negotiations
Mai ao krap; do not want, i.e. "no thank you"
Mai bpen rai; a laid-back attitude, it doesn't matter, never mind
Mai mee panha; no problem
Maleng; an insect, whether edible or not
Mamasan; brothel madam
Maw; doctor
Mia chao; rented wife
Mia glang tasee; slave wife
Mia luang; principal (legal) wife
Mia noi; minor wife
Moo; pig
Moobaan; housing estate
Mun; it (derogatory)
Nai luang; the respectful term for H.M.King Bhumibol, Rama IX
Naklaeng dto; a gangland leader

Nam; water
Nam jai; giving and sharing
Nam mon; holy water sprinkled by monk
Nawng; a younger person
Oun; fat
Pa; aunt
Pai nai krap; where are you going?
Paradorn; fraternity
Parsa racharap; royal language
Pee; an older person
Phak puak; social circle of friends
Phra hat; hand (royal language)
Phra phak; face (royal language)
Pitak Siam; a political faction with some prominence in 2012
Ponsawadarn; history, story of the kings
Poo dee angkrit; polite and reserved person
Poo mee itthipon; mafia godfather
Poo peepaksa; respectful term for a judge
Poot mark mark; you talk too much
Pootwan; sweet talk
Prachut; anger directed at a person other than the real antagonist
Prai; serfs, plebs; contrast with the ammart or élite
Prungnee; tomorrow
Punoi; person of low status
Puyai; person of high status, a superior
Puyaibaan; village headman
Ramvong; Thai traditional dance
Rot dai mai kap? can you give me a small discount?
Ruam took ruam sook; sharing the good and the bad times
Sai sin; white cord put round your wrist by a monk as a blessing
Sakdina; early system of tax collection

Sala; temple meeting hall, also an open and shady pavilion in a garden
Sam nuk bun kun; reciprocal giving
Samsara; the Buddhist cycle of cause and effect
Sangha; the Buddhist church
Sang katan; ceremony of merit in front of a monk
San phra bhumi; spirit house
Sanuk; fun
Satang; a low value Thai coin
Satang rawn; corrupt or hot money
Sat nam; water ceremony at a funeral
Sawatdee krap; sawatdee ka; the word for both hello and goodbye in Thai
Sawng phra ja rern; long live the king
Sawngtaew; two-bench open taxi
See moong chao; 10 am in the morning
See tum; 10 pm in the evening
Sin nam jai; a goodwill gift, a type of bribe
Sin sot; wedding dowry
Soi; lane, small road
Somrak; proper love
Sutras; holy scriptures
Tabian baan; house registration document
Talapatr; traditional fan held by a monk
Talay; sea
Tambon; merit (also the word for district)
Tambonbaan; house warming
Tambon roi wan; funeral rite 100 days after death
Tee see; 4 am in the morning
Tuk jai, mai tuk tong; all heart, not all correct
Tura mai chai; it's not my concern
Upakka; being calm in difficult situations

Wai; the Thai form of greeting with the hands in a prayer-like position
Wan wai kroo; teachers' day
Wanna; boss
Wat; temple

Printed in Germany
by Amazon Distribution
GmbH, Leipzig